SEE-THROUGH
HOUSES

SEE-THROUGH
Catherine Slessor
HOUSES
INSPIRATIONAL HOMES AND FEATURES IN GLASS

Photography by **James Morris**

RYLAND
PETERS
& SMALL

London New York

SENIOR DESIGNER **Paul Tilby**
SENIOR EDITORS **Sophie Bevan, Henrietta Heald**
LOCATION AND PICTURE RESEARCH MANAGER
Kate Brunt
PICTURE RESEARCHER **Jenny Drane**
PRODUCTION DIRECTOR **Meryl Silbert**
ART DIRECTOR **Gabriella Le Grazie**
PUBLISHING DIRECTOR **Alison Starling**

ILLUSTRATOR **Russell Bell**
PROJECT EDITOR **Anthea Snow**
PROOFREADER **Nikky Twyman**
INDEXER **Diana Le Core**

First published in the USA in 2001 by
Ryland Peters & Small, Inc.
519 Broadway
5th Floor
New York, NY 10012
www.rylandpeters.com

10 9 8 7 6 5 4 3 2 1

Library of Congress Cataloging-in-Publication Data

Slessor, Catherine.
    See-through houses : inspirational homes
and features in glass / Catherine Slessor ;
photography by James Morris.
       p. cm.
    Includes index.
    ISBN: 1-84172-029-1
    1. Glass construction. 2. Architecture,
Domestic. 3. Glass in interior decoration. I.
Morris, James. II. Title.

NA7186 .S58 2001
721`.04496--dc21

              2001031778

Jacket credits
All photographs by James Morris. *Front:* Skywood House
near London designed by Graham Phillips. *Back, clockwise
from top left:* Joan Barnett's house in West Hollywood,
designed by William R. Heffner AIA, interior design by Sandy
Davidson Design; A loft apartment in London designed
by Simon Conder Associates; A house in London designed
by Rick Mather Architects; A mountain house in Georgia
designed by Mack Scogin Merrill Elam Architects

Printed and bound in China

CONTENTS

INTRODUCTION

Crystalline and ethereal, glass is one of the most magical materials on earth. It reveals space and transmits light, energizing and animating architecture. This book explores how the versatility of glass has been harnessed in the design of a remarkable series of houses drawn from around the world.

The history of glass is intimately linked with the evolution of architecture. In the thousands of years since humans learned to build, architects and designers have struggled to reconcile the need for enclosed shelter, protection, and privacy with the desire for illumination and views. Glass seemed the preordained answer to the apparently insoluble dilemma of how to devise a material that was transparent, durable, and strong, yet also economical to produce.

Although glass has been used in buildings for over a thousand years, its relationship with humankind dates back much farther. The invention of glass took place almost by accident, around 4,000 years ago in the eastern Mediterranean. Beneath an ancient pottery kiln, the fused silica of pots combined with the alkaline ash of the hearth below. By 1500 B.C., molded and pressed glass vessels were commonplace in Egypt, and the skills needed to make them had spread to Europe. The expansion of the Roman Empire lead to the establishment of a thriving glass industry in the provinces of Sâone and Rhine, employing craftsmen from Syria and Alexandria. The Latin term *glesum* (from a Germanic word meaning transparent or lustrous) was used to describe this versatile substance.

It took 2,000 years from the initial serendipitous discovery to the appearance of blown glass, which then led to the production of thin transparent sheets strong enough to be used for windows. Window glass production using blown cylinders began in northern Europe around the 11th century. The

Wood-framed glass walls give the interior of this rural retreat a lightness and transparency. The thin glass membrane dissolves the boundary between inside and out as the house merges with the landscape.

technique involved the blowing of a large cylinder, which was cut, opened out, and flattened. During the 1830s, an improved version of the traditional cylinder process began to be used more widely, providing glass of uniform thickness in sizes up to 3 x 4ft (1 x 1.3m). Until then, manufacturing techniques had restricted pane size, as shown by the intricate divisions of mullions and transoms in windows of the 18th and early 19th centuries. Such technical advances marked the beginning of a symbiosis between glass and buildings. As Michael Wigginton notes in *Glass in Architecture* (Phaidon, 1996): "With this development, new conceptual languages in architecture became possible, which are still being developed and explored; from the simple provision of light and view without a loss of warmth, to the creation of conceptual and technical masterpieces which derived their essential quality from this wonderful material."

Glass has not only protected and served us, but has also given rise to the sublime glories of the Gothic cathedral and the functional beauty of the 19th-century conservatory and glazed galleria. The pioneering architects of the Modern Movement were the first to exploit the potential of glass to achieve a new fluidity of space and transparency of enclosure. Writing in 1931, the great German architect Walter Gropius asserted that "It can mark the limits to spaces, it can protect us against the weather, but at the same time opens up spaces, it is light and incorporeal."

house can allow an architect the range of creative expression that one might only associate with larger public buildings. Enlightened patronage is crucial to this process. All the clients whose houses are described here have given architects a free reign to exercise their imaginations. The outcome is a memorable and inventive series of buildings.

For the clients, the object is to create a place of shelter and stimulation; for the architects, the house is both talisman and testing ground. Despite social and cultural changes, the basic requirements an owner looks for in a house remain essentially unchanged. This near-sacred simplicity of the house also makes it perhaps the only building type for which an architect can give full vent to his or her creativity and can exercise complete design control and establish a genuinely intimate client relationship. Transformed into a vehicle for personal expression for both client and architect, the house comes to represent the fulfillment of dreams.

The notion of glass as a beautiful material in its own right was a key tenet of early 20th-century Modernism, which finds continued expression in the work of contemporary architects and designers. Yet the increasing sophistication of glazing technology means that its use is not confined to the exterior. Powerful contrasts between light and shadow, opacity and transparency can be realized through the skillful use of glass in walls, screens, floors, and staircases.

Glass resolved a dilemma: how to devise a material that was transparent, durable, and strong, yet also economical.

Throughout history, glass has driven architecture to great conceptual heights, but its use in more commonplace buildings, such as private houses, should not be overlooked. These have also proved a stimulus to architectural and technical imagination, as this book demonstrates. Because of their relatively small scale, houses offer fertile scope for experimentation. Today, architecture has witnessed a strong return to the concept of the small private villa, and given the right sort of client, a commission for a private

The range of glass now available—translucent or clear, textured or colored—can create a compelling variety of effects, depending on the character of the space.

This book celebrates the relationship between glass and contemporary house design. Prefaced by a section on pioneering glass architecture, the chapters that follow are thematically organized around a series of case studies, and the final chapter focuses on glass in interior design. Many of the buildings shown represent the fulfillment of technical and aesthetic ambitions first postulated by the Modern Movement; yet, as the new century begins, such ambitions continue to engross architects and designers.

A house in the forests of Maine reinterprets the traditional form of local farmhouses based on a series of clustered elements. Glass plays a crucial role in opening up the house to light and views.

The capture and manipulation of light has always been integral to architecture. By shaping buildings to receive and display solar movement, the mobility of the skies was revealed and drawn into buildings. The development of glass has played a key part in this quest for lightness and transparency.

In 1914, German visionary writer Paul Scheerbart described his fantasy of a world revitalized by glass architecture "which lets in the light of the sun, the moon and the stars, not merely through windows, but through every possible wall, which will be made entirely of glass." Scheerbart vividly expressed a dream that proved an inspiration to the emerging Modern Movement at a time when the potential of glass technology was newly revealed. Today, his vision of an architecture made entirely of glass is rapidly becoming a reality, propelled by technical advances allied to the fertile power of architectural imagination.

Perched on the edge of a Los Angeles hillside, John Lautner's spectacular Sheats-Goldstein House (1963) combines all the comforts of the 20th century with the reassuring primeval metaphor of the cave. The monolithic roof slab is articulated by the sculptural pattern of triangular coffers cast into the concrete. During the day, light streams through small glass roof lights.

Historically, the relationship between glass and architecture is at its most sophisticated when transcending technical limitations, notably those imposed by load-bearing masonry construction that restricted the width of window openings.

The first breakthrough was the Gothic exoskeleton; the stone frames and flying buttresses of medieval cathedrals made possible unprecedentedly tall, arched windows composed of jewellike fragments. The next quantum leap occurred in the 19th century with the introduction of the skeletal structural frame, initially fabricated from cast and wrought iron, later from steel and reinforced concrete. Victorian iron and glass technology led to a new architectural language and new typologies: conservatories, arcades, heroic glazed train sheds, and exhibition buildings, notably Joseph Paxton's seminal Crystal Palace of 1851 in London, which used over 300,000 sheets of glass.

In the 20th century, Le Corbusier's canonical description of architecture as "the masterly, correct and magnificent play of masses brought together in light" affirmed a new set of values for modern buildings: transparency and dematerialization, achieved through material lightness and spatial interpenetration. The symbolism of glass and metal gradually found new

expression in the form of a glass skin, as opposed to glazed openings in a skeletal structure. Walter Gropius's Fagus Factory of 1911 was one of the first examples of a glass facade supported by a thin steel framework; Bruno Taut's polygonal Glashaus Pavilion for the 1914 Werkbund Exhibition in Cologne was made entirely from glass, dramatically celebrating its ephemeral, crystalline properties.

The 1920s witnessed an extraordinary exploitation of glass in the pursuit of the new aesthetic of transparency and dematerialization. Houses and small projects by pioneering architects such as Mies van der Rohe demonstrated the change of attitude sweeping across Europe and the United States after World War I. Both the Tugenhadt House (1930)—a huge villa in the Czech town of Brno—and the Barcelona Pavilion—built for the 1929 International Exhibition—were inspired by the quest for free-flowing space and minimal enclosure. The only way to achieve this was through using glass with as little interruption from the frame as possible. The term "picture window" is derived from this view of glazing exemplified by the Tugenhadt House, in which the windows could be lowered electrically and removed. Its cost was phenomenal (equivalent to eight luxury apartments), but it showed what could be achieved.

Another seminal glass house, but executed in a totally different context, was Pierre Chareau's Maison Dalsace completed in 1931. Unlike the Tugenhadt House, which took the form of a villa on a plot, the Maison Dalsace is tucked into a courtyard in Paris's Latin Quarter and retains the second-floor apartment of an existing tenant above. Chareau's solution uses a steel structure to support a wall of glass blocks.

In America the potential of technology in general, and glass in particular, created a new spirit that paralleled developments in Europe. Frank Lloyd Wright

"Glass is the purest form of building material made from earthly matter." (Gropius, 1931)

caught the mood in 1930: "Shadows were the brush work of the ancient architect. Let the modern now work with light, light diffused, light reflected, light for its own sake, shadows gratuitous. It is the machine that makes modern these new opportunities in glass." Architects such as Mies van der Rohe (by then settled in the U.S.) and Philip Johnson strove to explore the potential of transparency and the all-glass skin. Mies's masterpiece was the Farnsworth House (1946–51), one of architecture's greatest minimal statements. Two identical rectangular planes of floor and roof are held above each other by steel columns. The glass walls seem almost superfluous, serving only to mediate between the outside world and the occupied space within. It is the supreme pavilion in the

landscape. Johnson's own house in New Canaan, CT, completed in 1949, clearly shows the Miesian influence. Core elements are restricted to a sculptural cylindrical drum containing a shower room and fireplace; the rest of the amorphous space is enclosed by glass.

Both these houses form an intriguing contrast with another contemporary glass house, designed and built by Charles and Ray Eames at Pacific Palisades in California, as part of the Case Study House Program, initiated by *Arts & Architecture* magazine. Born during a period of optimism and anticipation after years of economic depression and war, the program offered architects the chance to develop new prototypes for family housing, incorporating new materials and new

LEFT AND FAR LEFT **Pierre Chareau's Maison Dalsace, known as the Maison de Verre (House of Glass) was built in 1931 for a Paris doctor. It incorporates a steel structure supporting a soaring wall made of translucent blocks. Like a *shoji*, or Japanese rice-paper screen, in which light is filtered through a diaphanous membrane, the shimmering skin provides the double benefits of light and privacy.**
FAR LEFT, ABOVE **Despite its extreme abstraction, Mies van der Rohe's Farnsworth House (1946–51) remains a powerful conceptual model.**
ABOVE **Philip Johnson's house in New Canaan, completed in 1949, is a fluid space enclosed by an apparently insubstantial glass skin.**

conditions. Neutra's Kaufmann House (1946) is a sanctuary in the Palm Springs desert from which to savor the elemental power of the surrounding landscape. Its glass walls slide back to blur the distinction between the interior and exterior realm, emphasizing the free-flowing character of the space. Koenig's iconic Case Study House 22 (1960) is a crisply detailed glass pavilion clinging vertiginously to a steep hillside, with the grid of Los Angeles receding below. The same spirit of lightness and connection with nature informs the recent work of Glen Murcutt in Australia. The house built by Lautner in 1963 for the Sheats family is like a cave made of 20th-century materials. Again, it nestles into a hillside overlooking the panoramic splendour of Los Angeles. Lautner's bold geometry, his technological skill and his notion of architecture as fluid space might identify him as a follower of Modernism, but his maverick sensibility and his concern for quality of life sets him apart.

With its inherent conservatism and less clement climate, Britain has been more resistant to the notion of glass houses. Those that have been built tend to be architects' own dwellings, such as John Winter's striking house in Highgate, north London (1969), which combines a deliberately rusted steel frame with sheer glass walls, and the industrially inspired, steel and glass kit-of-parts house by Michael and Patty Hopkins in Hampstead (1977). Completed in 1969, the house Richard Rogers designed for his parents is an evocative reminder of the expressive power of minimal architecture. Two single-story glass pavilions are carefully arranged along a deep garden plot, creating a world of supreme tranquillity and order within the bourgeois London suburb of Wimbledon. More recently, Future Systems completed a stunning private house in Canonbury, north London (1994), which inventively combines a street frontage of translucent glass blocks with a dramatic sloping glass wall to the rear. Constructed from 22 panels of thermally efficient, silicone-sealed double glazing,

techniques of prefabrication that had been originally developed for wartime use. Conceived with great idealism, it was underpinned by the hope that these experiments in technology-centered housing would lead to a greater public acceptance of the principles of Modernism.

The Eames House, which contained living and working accommodation for the couple, became the symbol of the program. Set in a lushly landscaped site, its stark steel frame is clad in a precisely articulated grid of colored panels, like a Mondrian painting. Windows are filled with panels of transparent, translucent, and wired glass. As it was intended to be an off-the-shelf building, the Eameses used small, steel-framed windows, already on the market, following their philosophy of selecting well-designed industrial products and putting them together to create light, elegant, and accommodating architecture.

The equable West Coast climate, readily available land, new technologies, and a generation of architects eager to experiment gave rise to the remarkable glass houses of California Modernism. Architects such as Pierre Koenig, Albert Frey, John Lautner, Craig Ellwood, and Richard Neutra reveled in such

ABOVE AND RIGHT **Designed in 1963 by John Lautner as a symbol of the hedonistic California lifestyle, the Sheats-Goldstein House was recently remodeled. Floor-to-ceiling frameless glass encloses the bedroom eyrie, offering views of the Los Angeles city lights below.**
ABOVE LEFT **The living room is enclosed by a concrete roof slab punctured by hundreds of tiny roof lights made from upturned drinking glasses.**
LEFT AND FAR LEFT **Clean lines, bold forms, and simple materials distinguish the work of a master architect. Contact with nature is also important, and the house's leafy, dramatic site is visible through a sheer glazed skin.**

Advances in glass technology offer new ways of using transparency and lightness in the quest for formal invention.

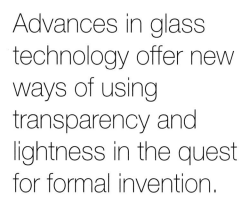

the four-story wall cascades down at an angle of 50 degrees, giving the occupants not so much an unimpeded view of the outside world as the illusion of actually living in the air.

The increasing sophistication of glass and of lightweight transparent plastics since the 1980s has offered architects enriched possibilities. The synergetic combination of a steel structure and the inherently tensile qualities of glass has advanced contemporary ideals of lightness and transparency, but another line of inquiry goes further, by exploiting

ABOVE LEFT, TOP, AND ABOVE
In Britain, the most striking glass houses are frequently those built by architects for themselves, such as this kit-of-parts house created by Michael and Patty Hopkins in Hampstead, north London. Its formal economy and spatial flexibility have a clear Modernist lineage, showing the potential of combining steel-framed constructional systems with glass walls to develop a dynamic domestic architecture. The Hopkins House has an adaptable interior featuring movable partitions, hard-edged, workmanlike materials, and bold primary colors.

the properties of glass in compression. The outcome is the glass column and the glass beam, used in such projects as Rick Mather's highly unusual extension to a heritage house in north London (1993). Exuding a Miesian simplicity and a seamless transparency, the glazed skin is supported by a laminated glass structural frame. Such projects herald the tantalizing possibility of the ultimately transparent enclosure.

Another important aspect of the development of glass buildings is the emergence of environmentally responsive design. (Despite its progressiveness, the Eames House, for instance, was difficult to regulate environmentally; when asked by a visiting architect how it was heated, Charles pointed to the sweater he was wearing.) Many of the most innovative projects have been produced for private houses, as they form a tangible starting point for prototypical solutions. In Germany in particular, "green" awareness is high,

reflected in the domestic work of architects such as Log ID and Thomas Herzog, which incorporates active and passive environmental control measures, using glass conservatories and photovoltaic panels to generate energy from sunlight. In Britain, Bill Dunster's recent Hope House in East Molesey (1995) continues this vein of ecologically aware investigation, the results of which will be used in the design of future schemes for sustainable, high-density urban housing.

Writing in 1931, Walter Gropius presciently observed: "Although glass as such has been known to us for many years, it is the technical age we now live in with all its modern manufacturing processes that has rendered this substance one of the most valuable materials of our day and of the future. Glass architecture, until recently deemed purely utopian, is now a reality."

ABOVE **The work of Australian architect Glen Murcutt is informed by a spirit of material lightness. His houses seem to mesh with the nearby bush, their glass walls protected by overhanging roofs made of corrugated metal. His Bell-Eastaway House at Glenorie (1983) was inspired by the functional directness and simplicity of farm buildings.**
RIGHT **A curved corrugated-steel roof encloses a decking terrace, shielding the sheer glass walls from the glare of the sun. Basic materials are used inventively and discreetly to create simple, elegant dwellings that sit lightly on the ground.**

The current fascination with material and spatial lightness in homes is nowhere better illustrated than in the use of glass—and translucent or transparent materials—in architecture. The quest for transparent perfection has moved on from the simple glass box that attracted early Modernists to the more subtle and diffuse notions of contemporary architects, reflecting the increasing sophistication of building technologies. Now technology and imagination can be combined with apparently limitless possibilities. The development of lightweight steel-frame construction to replace heavy, load-bearing walls has encouraged the use of glass on a larger and more ambitious scale. New methods of producing glass and anchoring sheets in position further heighten the potential for invention. The unique and important quality of glass is its ability to transmit daylight. Sheer glass walls bring light into space, dematerializing the boundaries between inside and out, bringing the occupants into an intimate relationship with their surroundings. The crisp lines of glass houses often form a striking contrast with the lushness and color of the landscape. Like a tantalizingly ephemeral mirage, buildings appear to float and dissolve, hovering lightly, their walls barely there.

Ken Shuttleworth designed this house around a gently curving glass wall. The glazed crescent infuses the interior with light and opens up the house to the surrounding landscape, bringing nature into the heart of domestic life. The croissant-shaped living room is formed around views and light.

Skywood: planar simplicity

ARCHITECT: **GRAHAM PHILLIPS**

This exquisitely simple house transforms domestic life into a work of art—a feat both demanding and rewarding. It was demanding because to achieve such heightened and successful visual refinement involved enormous perseverance and dauntingly complicated construction. Each artefact was carefully selected and meticulously positioned, but the outcome—which combines practicality with aesthetic triumph—was definitely worth the effort. The architect of this impressive work was Graham Phillips.

At first sight, Skywood appears to belong to the familiar tradition of lightweight, steel-framed houses that arose from the postwar Case Study House Program in California. It has none of their informality, however, making less of its steel frame and more of its walls, sheer white planes that extend out in a pinwheel and end up in the landscape, like those of Mies van der Rohe's Brick Country House of 1924. In their close relationship with water, the walls also owe a debt to Luis Barragán's work in Mexico. But Phillips's most powerful and primal model was that of the villa, reinterpreted for modern life, as in Le Corbusier's iconic Villa Savoye built in 1931 in a meadow in suburban Poissy, just outside Paris. The purity of such a building produced the clearest definition of a strand of Modernism that sees architecture not as a collage of decoration, but as a distillation of all domestic functions into an abstract form, contained within a precise, geometric whole.

The owner's many years of searching in the London area finally culminated in the discovery of a remarkable site: 4.5 acres (1.8 hectares) of profusely overgrown

LEFT **The side of the house is lapped by a tranquil artificial lake, so it appears to be floating on the water. The aim was to create a glass box in the woods, breaking down the boundaries between inside and outside.**
INSET **The glass walls open up the house to its setting, framing views of the landscape.**
BELOW **After winding through woodland, the approach to the house terminates in a Zenlike entrance courtyard, inset with black gravel.**

ancient woodland with huge mature rhododendrons and an existing house suitable for demolition. Zoning restrictions and a tree-preservation area meant that the new house could be no more than 2,700 sq ft (250 sq m) overall floor area and had to fit in with the existing mature tree pattern. The architect's original intention had been to create a glass box in the woods, but this evolved to include water as a key element and to explore the house's wider relationship with the landscape.

The carefully staged experience of discovery and arrival begins at the main gates. As you round the first bend of the black gravel drive, the house appears in a breathtaking vista set at the far end of a linear lake. You then drive through the gloomy, luxuriant woods before re-emerging over a bridge in the main entrance court at the rear of the house. At the bridge, the source of the water is revealed as a simple black obelisk running with aerated water. Paved with flush gray limestone slabs inset with a black gravel turning circle, the entrance courtyard forms part of

ABOVE **The house has to respond sensitively to its site, fitting in with the existing pattern of mature trees.**
ABOVE RIGHT **Living space is enclosed by a diaphanous glass membrane, designed to look effortless, but in fact a precise feat of engineering and construction.**
INSET **A crisply articulated geometry of solid and transparent wall planes is reflected in the lake.**
RIGHT **Interiors are minimally furnished to form a contrast with the richness and color of the setting.**

Enclosed by planes of transparent glass, the living room has an air of calculated asceticism enhanced by a simple yet elegant choice of furniture.

a huge stone plinth on which the house sits. The courtyard's deliberate austerity—no plants, garage doors, pipes, or gutters—emphasizes its simple, elemental form. Carport and entrance are enclosed by arbors made of red cedar that will eventually weather to a bleached silver color.

The plan of the house is based on a classic pinwheel form of long, high walls that extend beyond the enclosed spaces into the lake and landscape to define key site axes and pathways. The house is positioned so that it is never very clear where

nature ends and dwelling begins, dictated by the need to preserve trees and a desire to savor a long view through the garden, a vista now largely filled by the artificial lake. Each of the three great walls that shoots off from the house defines a very different place. The entrance court is austere. The compact entrance hall has minimal views out, but each-way internal vistas extend the full width of the house and make it seem impossibly large. This hall leads into the living room with its grand view along the lake and surrounding trees.

At the end of the lake is an island, which forms a focus by day, and also at night, when it is lit by external floodlights. The lake has a crisp straight edge, with a mown lawn on one side and unmanicured woodland on the other, where reeds will be encouraged

ABOVE RIGHT **A cantilevered canopy protects the glass walls from overheating and the sun's glare, casting a delicate lattice of shadows on the terrace overlooking the lake.** ABOVE FAR RIGHT **The dining area offers stunning views of the lake. The precise geometry and sleek, simple forms recall the innovation and optimism of early Modernist houses.** RIGHT **The glass wall seems barely there, reduced to its merest essence. The landscape surrounding the house forms a constantly changing seasonal backdrop to domestic life.** BELOW RIGHT **Space is fluidly planned to take advantage of light and views. Dining and living areas merge seamlessly together in a single luminous room. Narrow strips of clerestory glazing admit more light and create the impression that the roof is hovering unsupported.**

Bathed in light that floods through the glass walls, the interiors are simple white spaces, enriched by the landscape and shimmering lake.

to grow. On the other side of the entrance hall, a block of bedrooms overlook their own tranquil inner court, with a magnolia tree and lawn.

Living spaces are contained within two pure rectangular forms enclosed by frameless glass. The main communal space is a double square, with the living area defined by a change in floor texture, from limestone to carpet, echoing the inlays and changes of texture in the courtyard and rear garden. The fireplace alcove ingeniously integrates a television, fireplace, and log store in a continuous black slot. In the kitchen–dining zone, flexibility is the key, with a set of full-height sliding and folding partitions and two movable tables that allow a quick and efficient change from an open-plan family kitchen arrangement with a linear bench, to a more formal square dining table in the center of the room, with the kitchen counter screened from view.

Living areas face west and sleeping spaces face east. Each has a totally solid wall on one side and a transparent skin of fixed glazing on the other. It looks extremely simple, but requires extensive top lights to make it work: the bedrooms are ventilated by mechanically operated skylights, and the difference in height between the bedroom wing and the living part

of the house is made up by a clerestory, so the roof appears to float. White and blue lights on top of storage units combine with daylight from all directions to give the interior the powerful, dramatic quality of a James Turrell installation. The bedroom block forms one side of a completely enclosed walled garden, with a perfect square of lawn set in a black gravel border. The intention is to grow ivy and vines on the inside surfaces of the garden walls to form a soft green enclave, a contrast to the hardness and austerity of the entrance court.

England has a powerful Arts and Crafts tradition based on the notion of celebrating construction and relishing how things are made. This house will have none of it. Instead, it is concerned with pure sensuous beauty; yet construction of considerable complexity and invention is used to achieve apparently simple forms. The roof, which looks like a flat slab, is in fact an intricate construction of steel and wood taking support where it can. The glazing, which looks so effortless, is a feat of engineering in itself, with a ⅝in (15mm) outer sheet bolted to the floor and cantilevering up to a sliding joint in the roof. An inner skin of low-emissivity glass gives a total thickness of 1⅝in (40mm). The outcome is a diaphanous, shimmering membrane, miraculously dissolving the boundaries between interior and exterior.

The simplicity of the house is achieved, in part, by designing out many of the normal building elements. There are no opening lights, no copings or drips, no visible switches, sockets, or hardware. Under-floor heating and the absence of heating grilles also reduce unnecessary clutter. Every detail is perfectly coordinated technically and geometrically within the

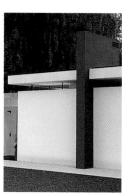

ABOVE **Incised into the landscape, a spine wall separates the main living quarters from the bedrooms. The house's effortlessly simple appearance belies the feat of complex construction and a faith in modern materials.**
BELOW **A detail of the external wall, clad in a sophisticated insulated white render that requires minimal maintenance and emphasizes the purity of architectural expression.**

fixed planning grid to achieve an entirely seamless appearance, a signature characteristic of this architectural firm. Even the kitchen faucet and kettle vanish obligingly behind sliding panels when not in use. Doors are set flush on both sides. The floor plane of the main area extends through the frameless glass skin, and the great planar walls retain the same thickness, virtually eliminating the distinction between the inside and the outside.

The entire composition is held together by a grid of the limestone floor slabs that run throughout the house. The resulting lack of visual distraction is a balm to the senses, prompting admiration of the effort that has been expended to achieve it. For instance, conventionally constructed walls obtain lateral stability from crosswalls or piers. Here they are required to be pure planes, necessitating reinforced concrete framing within the wall structure.

The 10ft- (3m-) high walls are clad in a sophisticated insulated render system that not only optimizes thermal performance, but also requires minimal maintenance, without the need for conventional copings, dampproof courses, or expansion joints that might compromise the absolute purity of the

architectural expression. The smooth white wall planes are reminiscent of the pioneering prewar houses of English Modernists such as F. R. S. Yorke and Maxwell Fry, who delighted in pure, Cubist forms and took advantage of the sculptural capabilities of concrete (at that time an exciting new material) combined with large areas of glass to create a radical new kind of light, open dwelling. The modern house of the 1930s leaked and cracked in a very short time, but current building technologies are much better able to resist the ravages of the English weather and have greatly advanced the quest for formal purity.

Like most architectural commissions, the brief was an evolutionary process. The initial intention, to create a magical glass house in a woodland setting and to maximize the sense of dematerialization of the boundaries between inside and outside, grew to encompass other issues, such as the desire to see the house at a distance and for bedrooms relating to a more private, softer, walled garden. All these aspects have been memorably resolved in the final design. With its skillful handling of space, light, and materials, Skywood is clearly a great achievement. More than that, it is a genuinely modern masterpiece.

BELOW **Detailing of walls and floors is elegantly seamless.**
BOTTOM LEFT **A long corridor with views to the garden leads to the sleeping quarters.**
BOTTOM RIGHT **Bedrooms overlook a secluded walled garden, generating a sense of intimacy and tranquility. Ivy and vines will cover the walls, creating a lush green enclave, a contrast to the hardness of the entrance court.**

THIS PICTURE The kitchen and dining areas are separated by a screen that can be folded back to extend the space.
FAR RIGHT Reflections cast magical patterns on the lake.
BELOW Magnified and mirrored by the glassy water, the house glows with an extraordinary radiance after dark.

A luminous pavilion

ARCHITECTS: **BATAILLE & IBENS**

This family house by the Belgian partnership of Bataille & ibens exploits techniques of prefabrication to generate a flexible living environment. Infused with a spirit of industrial functionalism, the design is based on a lightweight steel-framed structure, modular planning, and a system of movable partitions, which easily and efficiently allows for spaces to change and evolve as family needs dictate. Inspired by industrial-systems building, this formal economy and spatial flexibility has a clear Modernist lineage, from the iconic Eames House in California to more recent architects' own dwellings, such as Michael and Patty Hopkins' house, built in London during the mid-1980s. Although the sites were very different—the Eameses built on a suburban plot, while the Hopkinses colonized an inner-city rowhouse—both houses demonstrated the potential of simple steel-framed constructional systems combined with glass walls to create a dynamic new form of domestic architecture.

Surrounded by woodland, the Bataille & ibens site lies in a pleasant suburban district of Antwerp. Like most of the surrounding houses, the new dwelling adopts the typology of the villa on a plot, but its enigmatic translucence and reductivist composition give little away from the outside. It could, for instance, be easily mistaken for a small office or industrial workshop. From the street, the house appears as a crisply articulated flat roof hovering lightly over the entrance. Made from panels of corrugated steel, the flat roof is supported by slender steel columns. The roof canopy extends to create a carport, sheltering the entrance and conveying a sense of arrival. Walls of milkily translucent glass conspire to screen the house from the street, but, rather than completely excluding the outside world, their translucence hints at and partly reveals the more private realm beyond.

ABOVE **The house is a glazed pavilion. Its modular steel frame expresses a strong industrial aesthetic, softened by the surrounding forest.**
LEFT **The main entrance, framed by translucent screen walls, encloses two small patios.**

Inspired by industrial functionalism, the house has a translucence and reductivist composition that give little away from the outside.

At the center of the building is a landscaped courtyard-cum-greenhouse largely taken up by a pool. Like a Japanese Zen garden, this forms the tranquil heart of the house, given over to the peace and stillness of nature. The courtyard model also evokes the Mediterranean patio, which brings light into deep-plan houses and acts as a climate modifier. Here, this traditional form is reinterpreted in a striking contemporary idiom. Two additional enclosed areas are created on the main street side, defined by the translucent glass screens.

Made up of a grid of nine structural bays, the plan is a simple rectangle, divided into two principal zones. A study, a quartet of children's and guest bedrooms, and the master bedroom with ensuite

bathroom are placed on the street side of the house, overlooking the two external patios. These are filled with plants, creating a lush green screen. The cellular bedrooms and study form a protective buffer zone to the main living area beyond.

The entrance hall leads directly to the internal water-filled patio. In deference to the cool northern European climate, the patio is not open to the elements; instead, a glass-walled cloister has been wrapped around it, providing the occupants with a continuous awareness of the presence of water and light at the heart of the dwelling.

Living, cooking, and dining spaces are placed on the more secluded side of the house, overlooking the garden. Each of these spaces is connected by

RIGHT The plan of the house adopts a traditional inward-looking patio form, with the main spaces arranged around a central enclosure. The model is the Mediterranean patio, which allows light to penetrate the deep-plan houses and helps to regulate temperature. The bedrooms, an ensuite bathroom, and a small study are on the entrance side, overlooking two more planted enclosures. Living, cooking, and dining spaces are on the more private side of the house, overlooking woodland. Each space is linked by a sliding glass door to a terrace, so that activities can extend outdoors. Based on a rectangular structural grid, the plan is intended to be highly flexible and fluid—partitions can be easily moved around to create different spatial relationships. Rooms dissolve informally into one another, enhancing the sense of openness.

Landscaped with a pool and carefully chosen plants, an enclosed patio forms the luminous heart of the house. Light is filtered through the glass walls and roof into the deep plan of the house. Furniture and fixtures are chosen to reflect the house's inventive, functional spirit.

OPPOSITE **Sliding glass walls mark the boundary between terrace and living space. The house demonstrates the potential of simple steel-framed constructional systems combined with glass walls to create an innovative form of domestic architecture that is simple and quick to construct and sits lightly in the landscape. This modular, kit-of-parts approach generates the ultimate flexibility. If the family should decide to move at some time in the future, the house can easily be dismantled and rebuilt in a new location.**

ABOVE **A functional yet elegant kitchen overlooks the backyard. Here and elsewhere in the house, pure lines and absolute simplicity reflect the architects' desire to distill architecture down to its bare but poetic essentials, allied to elegantly pared-down detailing.**
RIGHT **Entirely encased in glass walls, the house adapts and responds to the evolving demands of domestic life. The external skin is composed of a basic glazed modular panel that can function as either a door or a wall, creating the potential for future modification if needs change.**

sliding glass doors to a wood-decked terrace, so that activities can spill outdoors in warmer weather. The plan is intended to be highly flexible and fluid: mobile partitions can be easily moved around to create different spatial relationships.

The house thus forms an adaptable armature for the changing demands of domestic life. Rooms meld into one another, generating a sense of openness and lightness, a feeling enhanced by the water-filled patio and its glazed walls. Sparkling and scintillating in the sun, the pool reflects light and casts dappled shadows through the interior. Throughout the house, glass plays an important part in the strategy of transparency and spatial interpenetration. Apart from the concrete foundations, all of the structural elements were prefabricated off site and then slotted together. The lightweight steel frame supports a simple flat roof made of corrugated metal and detailed with functional precision. Walls are fashioned from a glazed modular panel that doubles as either a door or wall. This kit approach generates the ultimate flexibility. If the family decides to move, the house can simply be dismantled and rebuilt on a new site.

Searching for the power and sensuality of space, Bataille & ibens' work is boldly minimalist in its approach. Their aim is to forge a lucid connection between the underlying concept and the final building form and detailing, reducing architecture down to its pared-down minimum. In a world saturated with complex and conflicting imagery, they argue for a return to an approach in which the power of silence claims its rightful place. This calm, luminous, flexible house is a convincing example of their rigorous philosophy and a lyrical illustration of the Miesian mantra: "less is more."

Sitting lightly in the landscape, the crisply detailed glass pavilion provides a flexible framework for the daily ebb and flow of family life.

Translucence in the woods

ARCHITECTS: **BATAILLE & IBENS**

LEFT **From the entrance hall there are views through to the rear yard beyond.**
FAR LEFT **The dining area is lit by a glazed mansard roof.**
FAR LEFT, ABOVE **Translucent glass blocks make up the wall on the entrance side of the house.**
ABOVE LEFT **Light streams in through the glass roof, filtered by the canopy of beech trees.**
ABOVE **Clear glass set within the block wall offers occasional glimpses of the outside world.**
TOP **An extended steel frame forms an entrance colonnade around the house.**

The eastern edge of Belgium's Zenne valley contains some of the country's most attractive landscape. There, on a wooded site on the edge of suburbia, Bataille & ibens were commissioned to design a large family house. Their response was decidedly unconventional in terms of both form and materials. As with a previous house outside Antwerp (see pages 30–37), the architects showed their preference for a tautly functional architectural spirit, inspired by the simplicity and rigor of industrial buildings, but allied to a sensual handling of light and space.

They combined a structural steel frame with glass to achieve a crisply detailed pavilion that sits lightly yet elegantly on the ground. Despite its rural setting, the house boldly embraces an urban, quasi-industrial aesthetic. Everything is simple, unadorned, and explicit; constructional details are lucidly expressed, and refreshingly, there is no attempt to design a bland pastiche of a typical Belgian country villa.

Set in a clearing in the woods, the house is a relatively modest single-story rectangular volume. It is supported by a structural steel frame that extends beyond the building line to enclose a carport. The steel frame also forms a narrow colonnade that marks the route to the entrance, celebrating the point of arrival. The rectangular plan is bisected across its width by an entrance hall that divides the main living space at one end from the cellular bedrooms and bathrooms at the other. Wrapping

around an island kitchen area, the living room is a fluid, open-plan space that is connected to a terrace at the back of the house.

The roof plane curves up to form an angled mansard roof covered in zinc and filled in with vertical panes of clear glass. Designed to maximize the transmission of light, the imposing mansard resembles the roof forms of artists' studios. It also creates additional height, so the living space is transformed into a tall, lofty volume with a gently curved ceiling. The sloping glass roof of the mansard captures daylight, which in summer is filtered through the thick canopy of the surrounding beech trees.

Above the bedrooms, the extra volume is used to form a mezzanine level overlooking the living area. Reached by a straight flight of stairs, the mezzanine contains a work space and library, providing a degree of seclusion from the main family spaces. The master bedroom and two children's bedrooms are placed at the rear of the house, looking out on a garden. Furniture and fixtures have a well-thought-out

ABOVE **A verdant scene is reflected in the kitchen window.**
RIGHT **Views out are veiled by a cataract of cloudy light, which transforms the interior into a luminous cocoon. Light filters through the diaphanous skin, but privacy is preserved. Panels of clear glass are set into the wall at certain points, to frame views.**

Diffusing light and preserving privacy, the glass block wall forms a gauzy veil around the house.

RIGHT **The mansard roof adds height, allowing the building of a mezzanine level above the bedrooms. The mezzanine overlooks the kitchen, dining, and living areas, and contains a work space and library. From this vantage point, the contrast between the transparent glass roof and the translucent block wall is clearly expressed. Light dapples in through both types of glass, animating the space.**

BELOW AND BOTTOM **Recalling an artist's studio, the glazed mansard roof enhances the transmission of light and increases the interior volume.** RIGHT **Bedrooms are placed on the house's more secluded side, overlooking a yard to the rear.** BELOW RIGHT **The living room is a fluid, open-plan space linked to an external terrace.** OPPOSITE **The glass-block wall acts like a translucent membrane in the manner of Japanese rice-paper screens. Despite being made of glass, the blocks have good insulating properties, so heat loss is minimized.**

refinement based on carefully chosen materials and a minimal color palette, consisting principally of grays and whites. Extending through the house in a seamless sweep is a floor of durable, dark-gray tiles that pick up the gray of the steel structure. Solid walls are painted white, but this austerity is softened by the pervasive greenery of the surrounding woods and landscape.

The two principal facades both incorporate glass, but in very different ways. At the rear, living space and bedrooms are covered in a transparent glass skin, enhancing the sense of contact with nature and giving views of the outdoors. On the entrance side, the wall is made of glass blocks that sheathe the house in a gauzily translucent membrane. Light filters through the diaphanous skin, but privacy is preserved.

Views of the outside are veiled by a cataract of cloudy light that transforms the house into a luminous cocoon. Occasional clear-glass panels are set into the wall to frame views—at the kitchen overlooking the entrance, for instance—but on this side of the house, the outlook is mainly of treetops seen through the clear-glass roof.

The use of glass blocks evokes Pierre Chareau's Maison Dalsace, also known as the Maison de Verre (House of Glass). Completed in 1931, it was one of the first buildings to realize the aesthetic as well as the functional potential in architecture of glass blocks. Tucked into a small courtyard in Paris's Latin Quarter, the house incorporates a steel structure supporting a huge wall made of translucent glass blocks, each one square and with a circular lens at the center. This shimmering skin provides both privacy, in a confined urban setting, and light, its softly glowing mass illuminating the courtyard in the evening. Bands of clear glazing offer glimpses of nature, engendering a sense of isolation and apartness from the world.

Glass blocks have an intriguing history that dates back to the beginning of the 19th century,

The austerity of glass and white-painted walls is softened by the pervasive greenery of the surrounding woods and landscape.

when glass "illuminators" were used to admit daylight into the interiors of ships and buildings. In St. Paul's churchyard in London, examples of circular glass slabs cast in stone or set within iron frames still exist as predecessors of the first modern glass blocks. In the early 20th century, metal-framed "pavement lights" appeared in the narrow alleyways of French and German streets, allowing much-needed natural light into the dingy, subterranean living quarters of staff and servants. Originally, blocks were made of solid

MAIN PICTURE **The roof curves up to increase the height of the living space. White walls and gray tiled floors provide a sober backdrop to daily domestic activities. The steel structure is exposed within the interior framing and defining space. Freestanding walls enclose the kitchen area, and simple yet elegant furnishings complete the picture.**
INSET **Signs of nature are never very far away, creating a lush green screen around the house.**

glass, but in the mid-1930s Corning Glassworks, an American glassmaking firm, developed a block made of heat-resistant glass that was partially evacuated during production to form a hollow cavity.

By 1938, glass blocks were being mass-produced, formed by fusing together two halves of pressed glass with a partial vacuum between the two sections, providing not only a degree of transparency but insulation values comparable to that of modern insulated double-glazing units. Glass blocks became widely used in the 1950s and 1960s, and have recently experienced a revival in popularity. Today's blocks come in a variety of patterns, shapes, and sizes and, endowed with the flexibility of masonry construction, can be used to form external walls, as well as internal partitions and screens in a range of configurations, from simple orthogonal forms to more complex curved and serpentine designs.

The glass-block facade of the Brussels house resembles an apparition, an evanescent shimmer of glass set within the elegant lines of its steel grid. The veiling effect of the translucent blocks recalls the comment made to Le Corbusier by the great Austrian architect Adolf Loos that "a cultivated man does not look out of his window; it is there only to let light in, not to let the gaze pass through." Outer end walls are closed and opaque, as if decisively sealing off the light and transparency, like solid bookends. The fiber cement slabs covering the end walls have been sandblasted to achieve a more natural aging process, so the house will weather gracefully. The skeletal steel frame, which is painted dark gray, reinforces the impression of a tough yet expressive architecture that embodies a strong material inventiveness.

A minimal palette of white and gray forms a
neutral backdrop to the activities of family life.

Pastoral retreat

ARCHITECTS: **SIDNAM PETRONE GARTNER**

The wild landscape of upstate New York provides a refuge from the hectic pace of city life, and the retreat to an isolated spot in an untouched rural landscape remains a seductive proposition. For the architect, a commission to design a place of escape from urban pressures, where it is possible to feel close to nature's timeless cycles of growth, decay, and rebirth, may be a challenge of the most demanding and inspiring kind. In contrast to other types of commission, the architect must tactfully ignore any neighboring buildings in order to achieve the elusive and exhilarating sense of communing solely with the natural world.

The New York City-based firm of Sidnam Petrone Gartner was commissioned to design a house on a densely wooded site enriched with rocky outcrops and dramatic topography. The aim was to embrace and reflect the landscape and provide the clients with a haven from which to contemplate and experience nature. Rising up from a promontory, the house appears deeply rooted in the ground itself, emerging as an extension of the geological strata beneath it.

The change in levels across the site is exploited to create a series of living and sleeping spaces that lock together like a Chinese puzzle. The plan is based on an L shape. The shorter leg of the "L" houses bedrooms and a carport; the longer leg contains the living and dining spaces. At the intersection of the two legs, at the house's intermediate level, is an entrance hall. On this floor are the carport and the master bedroom, connected to a large external terrace. Three guest bedrooms occupy the upper level.

From the entrance hall, a staircase leads down into the main living area, a stunning double-height volume that is the spatial and social focus of the house.

Facing a rocky outcrop, this imposing fully glazed structure is like a modern version of a greenhouse. It contains a fluidly open-plan arrangement of living, dining, and kitchen spaces protected by a broad-brimmed sloping roof that encloses the entrance hall and master bedroom, and constitutes the dominant element in the landscape, easing the transition between the various levels.

At the northern end of the house, the second, smaller volume containing the guest bedrooms locks into the roof at right angles. This mass is counter-balanced at the southern end by a large chimney, which anchors the transparent skin of the living space while framing views of the rocky landscape beyond. The steel structure of the great room is left exposed, and in places is allowed to penetrate beyond the building envelope in order to heighten the distinction between the natural and the man-made.

Compared with the classic Miesian glass pavilion, with its rigidly orthogonal form and rigorously seamless construction, the geometry of this house is more relaxed and irregular. Corners are eroded to form windows; roofs are expressively angular; and the glazed skin of the main volume is composed of different-sized glass panels, creating the effect of

The soaring luminous volume of the living space is framed and surrounded by the lush profusion of nature. A steel structure supports the massive roof. Clear-glass panels of different sizes form a delicately transparent skin, separating the interior realm from the exterior. The drama is heightened by the contrast between the interior, with its elegant furniture, and the untamed surroundings. The house provides a civilized refuge from which to admire the changing seasons and the wildness of the landscape.

Enclosed by a soaring glass wall, the house provides a civilized refuge for the contemplation of nature.

LEFT **A sleekly minimal fireplace anchors the fluid living space. Classic Modernist furniture by Mies van der Rohe adds an air of civilized elegance.**
ABOVE, LEFT TO RIGHT **As the sun moves overhead, shadows dapple and animate the interior.**
RIGHT **Glazed surfaces are skillfully employed to focus and edit the way in which the surroundings are perceived from inside the house. The house is a contemporary response to the Modernist architectural tradition of using elements to frame and define views of the landscape.**
FAR RIGHT **The staircase is a crisply detailed composition of thin sheets of steel with a tensile wire balustrade. Its risers are formed from lightweight perforated steel sheets, so that light percolates through the structure. Antique candlesticks cluster around the fireplace, forming an evocative contrast between old and new.**

an informal mosaic. The roof is constructed from corrugated metal sheeting, a relatively cheap and functional material more commonly found on farm buildings and industrial structures.

Interiors are minimally furnished, with materials used elegantly and economically. Occupying pride of place in the living room are two classic Modernist chairs and a chaise longue originally designed by Mies van der Rohe. The ceremonial staircase leading down into the living space is a crisply detailed feature that would not be out of place in an inner-city loft. Thin sheets of steel are used to construct the stair treads, while the balustrade is made of tensile wires strung between steel uprights. The minimalist fireplace is surrounded by a cluster of antique candlesticks, making a striking visual and textural contrast. But the main furnishing is nature itself, pressing in on the glass walls with lush, uninhibited abundance. The house may have been conceived as an intimate, rural retreat, but it still boasts all the comforts of urban life.

The appeal of the pastoral ideal can be traced back to the 19th century, when ideas emerged about forging connections between home and landscape—whether by introducing artists' representations of the pastoral landscape into the home or, as in the Modernist architectural tradition, framing views of the landscape outside the house to be enjoyed from within. The result has been the evolution of strong concern to forge an exclusive relationship between the house and its surrounding natural context.

In this case, the great transparent wall assumes added significance and function, as the primary architectural medium of communication between internal space and nature beyond. By the skillful employment of glazed surfaces in order to frame, focus, and edit the way in which the landscape is perceived from inside the house, the architects have succeeded in heightening, dramatizing, and civilizing the profound and eternal relationship between man and nature.

ABOVE, LEFT TO RIGHT **The glass wall draws the garden into the house, while curved walls screen unsightly views and embrace the main entrance.**
BELOW **The house is designed around a gently bending glass wall enclosing the crescent-shaped living space.**
BELOW, FAR RIGHT **Tall doors open out onto the garden.**

Crystalline crescent

ARCHITECT: **KEN SHUTTLEWORTH**

Seen from afar at dusk on a winter's day, this house in the southern English county of Wiltshire shimmers through a veil of leafless trees. Its expansive, concave glass wall affords brief glimpses of the brightly lit living spaces within. The approach to the house is from the rear, however, where a solid curved white wall dominates, glowing eerily in the crepuscular light.

Gradually, the design is revealed. The plan resembles two croissants, one encircling the other, with entrances inserted at each end of a sliverlike intermediate space, which doubles as a gallery for art by the owners' children. The transparent glass crescent is oriented southeast toward the garden. The impervious white crescent is slightly different in its geometrical alignment, so the tall gallery between the two tapers in width from south to east. The main entrance is through a 10ft- (3m-) wide door under a concrete wall that doubles as a lintel.

All the activities associated with communal family life—cooking, eating, playing, sitting together—take place in the glass part of the house, elegantly contained within the continuous curved space, which opens up to the garden at each end. Bounded by

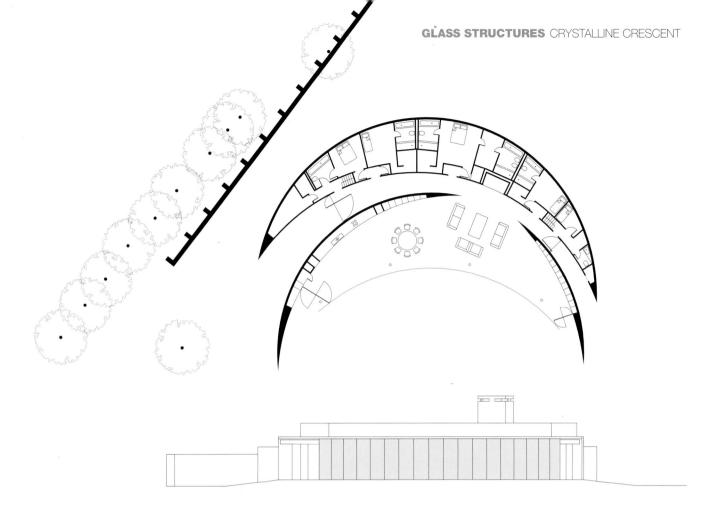

a 79ft- (24m-) long, concave, seamless facade of flat glass panels, this garden room wraps around a lawn. Roughly in the middle of the opposite wall is a break where the space opens across the clerestory-lit gallery to a huge fireplace.

The other crescent, which contains the bedrooms and bathrooms, is, in some ways, just as remarkable as the transparent section of the house. The bedroom crescent is windowless with just one long skylight along its outer edge, and all the beds are aligned so their occupants can lie looking up at the light of the moon and stars. These individual, private cells are intended to form a complete contrast to the flowing, curved space of the living area.

Concrete was chosen as the main structural material, mainly because there is a concrete plant just across the road, but also because the house needs to have a high thermal mass (in other words, to absorb and retain heat) to compensate for the large areas of glazing. Orientation of the glass wall was carefully adjusted to minimize solar overheating in summer and to take advantage of the best views. The elegant seamlessness of the wall is achieved by meticulous construction. Butt-edged glass panels are cantilevered from bolts at the base of the curtain wall, rising to a height of 13ft (4m).

The landscape design complements and reinforces the circular pattern implied by the plan. The inner crescent's glazed wall defines and embraces a round lawn clipped into a pattern of concentric rings. These circles overlap a larger hay and wildflower meadow, which in turn is bounded by a newly planted forest of deciduous trees. The house's pristine white exterior

ABOVE **The main garden elevation and the ground-floor plan illustrate the arrangement of the house, based on a pair of crescent-shaped forms set slightly skewed to each other, with a sliver of circulation space in between. The larger crescent contains the main living space, with the bedrooms placed to the rear. The living-room crescent opens up at each end, connecting with the garden.**
OPPOSITE, LEFT **A massive, pivoting door marks the threshold in the hallway.**
OPPOSITE, TOP RIGHT **Copious storage space is set within the depth of the wall that encloses the living room.**
OPPOSITE, BOTTOM RIGHT **Lit by bands of clerestory glazing, the curved hall acts as an informal gallery for the children's paintings.**

pays homage to traditional local farm buildings. The white is modified and tempered according to season: loose items such as towels, cushions, bedlinen, vases, and so on are changed in relation to the climate, so there is red for winter, yellow for spring, blue in summer, and green for fall. Clearly a good deal of discipline is required to live in such a house, but the compensation of being in such intimate contact with nature must make the effort worth attempting.

These fastidious set-dressing aspects of the project are underpinned by more pragmatic and profound ecological concerns. Despite the extensive areas of glazing, the house's energy consumption is the same as a standard three-bedroom dwelling, met by two compact compressors. There is also the potential to install solar panels and rainwater storage when such technologies become economically viable. This economy of energy usage has been achieved through the use of a concrete structure with masonry infill to provide a high thermal capacity and act as a heat store, so reducing extremes of temperature in the building. During the hottest part of a summer day, the house is shielded naturally by clusters of newly planted trees and light from the west is diffused through the entry gallery's clerestory windows. The interior benefits from cross-ventilation, and in warm weather the chimney acts as a passive ventilation stack; hot air rises naturally and is dispersed. The

The crescent-shaped form screens the surroundings and defines views.

All aspects of communal family life are elegantly contained within a continuous curved space enclosed by a seamless glass skin.

planting of 1,000 trees near the house was a conscious environmental ploy, not only to provide shade from solar glare in summer but also to reduce the chilling effect of wind.

Such considerations demonstrate a level of ecological awareness and responsibility toward the land that meshes with the less tangible, more spiritual sense of connection running through the project. The inspiration for Shuttleworth's design is close at hand in the surrounding landscape of this part of England.

The crescent shape of the house recalls the circular sarsen (local sandstone) formations characteristic of the sacred neolithic monuments of Stonehenge and Avebury nearby, and echoes the patterns of the mysterious circular ditches and causeways created long ago by Avebury's inhabitants. At the same time, however, the design also embraces the reality of modern rural life. The site lies on a fringe location, with bucolic landscape on one side, but industrial intrusions such as a refuse dump, recycling plant, and sewage works on the other. These features helped to dictate the sheltering, crescent form. The

ABOVE The glazed crescent infuses the interior with light and opens up the house to the surrounding landscape, bringing nature into the heart of domestic life. At one end of the croissant-shaped living room is a kitchen area.
LEFT Kitchen, dining, and living spaces are all contained in a continuous, curved sweep.
RIGHT The interior is painted white throughout, enhancing the play of natural light. Furniture is chosen for its understated modern elegance.

The white interior is modified and tempered according to the season, as loose items such as pillows and bedlinen are changed in a seasonal cycle of color. Family possessions arrayed in simple grids of storage units also provide visual animation; although the house embraces an aesthetic of minimalism, this is not a dwelling where possessions are shut out of sight. While the interior crescent, with its glazed concave wall, is essentially one room, the outer crescent contains the bedrooms, bathrooms, and dressing rooms, accessed from the central curved hall. Daylight filters into the hall from high windows, bathing the space in a delicate luminescence.

house sits in the worst corner of the site, turning its back on the industrial clutter and reaching out to take in long views across the garden to the hills. The crescent solution is like a medieval castle wall, with cells contained within the thickness of the wall. It supplies protection as well as privacy, while the concave crescent of clear glass warms the internal spaces, maximizes daylight, and enhances contact

with nature. The extreme transparency of the garden facade becomes particularly apparent when the interior is illuminated at night, revealing the white volume of the main living space.

The project also pays homage to another type of architecture—this time, one that is closer to the present—to the solar semicircular Modernist houses that Frank Lloyd Wright designed between 1944 and 1959. In Wright's houses, concave walls are oriented to the sun's angles; in Shuttleworth's solution, the concave glass wall faces south and southeast, so the communal living spaces receive ample morning light. In other respects, the house's white volumes and seamless, machinelike detailing also recall Le Corbusier's houses of the 1920s and 1930s. The relationship to the ground plane, however, is very different. Elevated on slender columns, or piloti, Corbusier's houses stand aloofly apart from their natural settings. The house, with its incised footprint, sits on the land gingerly and lightly, inextricably

A powerful sequence of circular motifs links the house inextricably to the land.

BELOW **Ingenious construction techniques were used to create the seamless effect of the glass crescent.**
RIGHT **The individual cells of the bedrooms form a complete contrast to the flowing, curved space of the living area. Bedrooms have no windows; instead, daylight is introduced through a continuous skylight on the outer rim of the curve.**
OPPOSITE, BELOW **No compromise has been forced in the practicality of the house: kitchen and dining areas are large, fluid spaces.**
OPPOSITE, INSET **A huge fireplace warms the living and dining areas and marks the center of the house.**

connected to it through a powerful sequence of circular motifs. In form and philosophy, it lies midway between the organic nature of Wright's work, expressed through earthy materials and forms, and Corbusier's splendidly isolated objects in space. It also refers to a highly contemporary architectural language, developing the crescent-shaped geometry initially explored in Foster & Partners' curved, bermed addition to the Sainsbury Centre for Visual Arts in East Anglia, completed in 1991, that almost seems to disappear into the ground. In both this project and the crescent-shaped house, fluid forms underscore a strong connection with nature and the recognition of the immemorial spiritual power of the land.

Although Shuttleworth's double crescent raises the question of whether function is subordinated here to art, with living spaces stuffed uncomfortably into the fragments of a circle, the unusual curved forms of the house apparently do not pose such problems for the inhabitants. Although strongly formalistic, the

house seems to demand no undue sacrifices in the interests of practicality. Moreover, everyday life is enhanced by a powerful kinesthetic experience; in other words, the body's perceptions as it moves through the space. This experience is enriched by the ways in which the overall arrangement connects the house, not only to its wider setting but also to its place in the history of architecture. Extending the heroic lineage of modern private houses, it is truly a remarkable achievement.

For those in a position to commission a house, the retreat to an isolated spot in an untouched rural landscape remains a seductive proposition. One of the key threads running through contemporary domestic architecture is the relationship of building to landscape. The idea of blending in and blurring the distinctions between inside and outside is a theme that has consistently inspired architects from the Modernist period, particularly Frank Lloyd Wright, whose Prairie houses are distinguished by organically inspired forms that seem to meld with the surrounding topography. Glass plays its part in opening up such houses to light and views, emphasizing the links with nature. Glazed openings frame and define views, drawing the landscape into the house. An equally influential model is the transparent pavilion in the landscape, so memorably realized by Philip Johnson and Mies van der Rohe in the early 1950s. Crisp, precise, and delicately ethereal, it has assumed an almost iconic status, evoking a civilizing human presence that confronts the wildness of nature. Tom Jestico's modern house in south London, adopts the model of the glass pavilion, but here the connection with landscape is more intimate, since the house is set in a walled garden.

Frank Lloyd Wright's influence finds current expression in the work of fellow Americans such as Mack Scogin Merill Elam Architects, whose houses are stunning rural retreats set in densely forested sites where nature's radiance is revealed at every season—as at this house built for an artist in Maine.

03 LANDSCAPEHOUSES

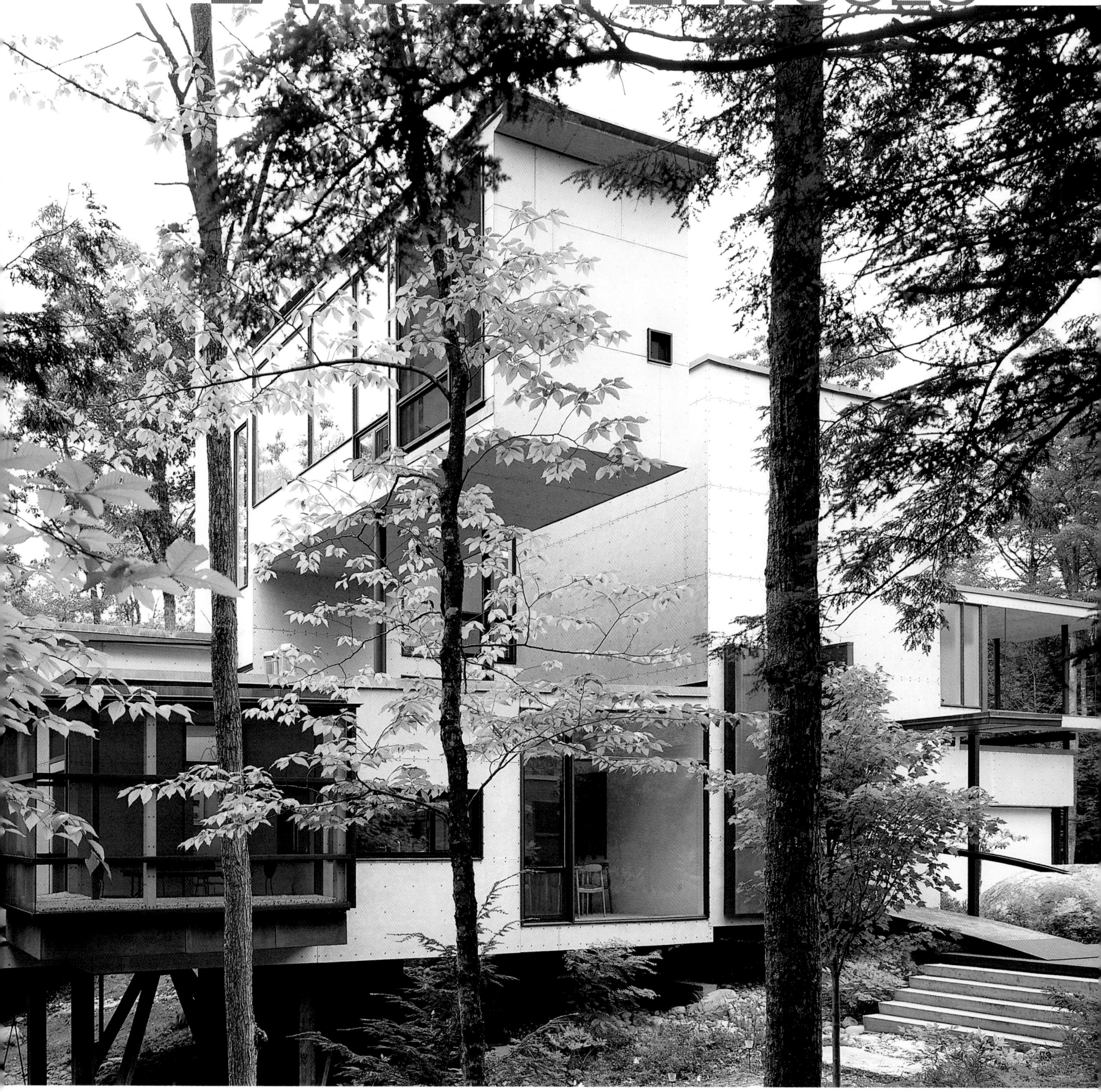

Ocean-going idyll

ARCHITECT: **MOORE RUBLE YUDELL**

California has an inventive tradition of private house design, forged by an equable climate, enlightened patrons, and architects eager to experiment. The Case Study House Program of the postwar era was a landmark in the evolution of the Californian private house, responding to location and to the individuality of the client. Ironically, it was originally intended to provide affordable modern housing types for low- and middle-income Californians, but—despite the success of the prototypes on an architectural level—American society had no means to provide mass housing, and most Angelenos still preferred tract bungalows. Rich Californians, however, got a new architectural aesthetic of transparent walls and flowing space, through which to express their lifestyles.

Some parallels can be drawn between attitudes to Modernism in the 1930s and developments in architecture in the 1990s, which saw a strong return to the small private villa. Now, with the right client, the private house can offer a level of experimentation and improvisation that might normally be associated with a larger public building. Moore Ruble Yudell is a leading American practice used to the challenges and collaborations of big projects, but the chance to return to a more modest scale and develop a more intimate client relationship proved hard to resist.

On the edge of the Pacific Ocean stands the Yorkin House, a luminous, tranquil oasis that turns its back on the blare and bustle of its surroundings. Designed by Buzz Yudell, John Ruble, and Marc Schoeplein, the house evolved in response to the constraints of its site. On one side, the nearby Pacific Coast Highway carries streams of traffic with attendant noise and distraction. On the other, sandy Pacific beaches provide a stunning and infinitely changing panorama of sand, light, and water.

The house forms an oceanside retreat for the owner, her two adult children, and their families. Open only to indirect light on the street side, it presents a largely hermetic face to the highway, in the manner of the traditional Mediterranean patio house, a model often reinterpreted in the California context. This aims to screen off the highway, creating a sheltered and serene inner realm. Animated by light scoops, the roof forms a habitable landscape for spectacular views and protection from breezes.

The structure unfolds as a series of layers that sustain a gentle transition from the intense and oppressive car culture outside. Entry is through a courtyard of native beach grasses over a wooden boardwalk, emphasizing the house's connection with nature and providing shelter and shade. Inside, there

ABOVE **Sea and sky are never very far away from the heart of the house.**
LEFT **Full-height glass walls connect the living spaces with the terraces, while sliding doors easily dissolve the boundaries between inside and outside. Overlooking the sea, the generous terraces evoke the decks of ocean liners. White walls and wooden floors reinforce the robust nautical spirit. A retractable canvas awning screens and diffuses the excesses of the sun's glare.**

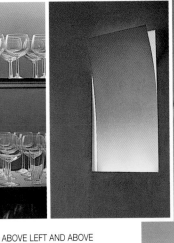

ABOVE LEFT AND ABOVE **Furniture and fixtures, including wall lights, have an understated elegance.**
RIGHT **A glimpse through to the kitchen reveals space unfolding in an informal series of layers, representing a gradual transition from the noisy highway on one side of the house to the calm of the ocean on the other.**
RIGHT, INSET **Framed views enhance a sense of spatial fluidity.**
OPPOSITE **The stairs at the core of the house are enclosed at upper level by panels of glass, diffusing light into the stairwell.**
OPPOSITE, INSET **Light casts abstract, shifting patterns throughout the interior.**

are many different sorts of spaces, from intimate family rooms to more transparent, open social areas that connect through sliding glass walls to an exterior courtyard, a terrace, and the beach beyond. Stairs weave vertically through this layered configuration, imparting color, light, and a sense of openness.

On the lower entrance level, the space is fluidly arranged, with living and dining areas forming an almost continuous volume. More workaday spaces such as the garage and laundry are placed on the highway side, acting as a buffer to the living areas beyond. On the second floor, bedrooms are hung like beads on a necklace off a spinal corridor. Only one bedroom and an exercise room are located on the road side, and the bedroom overlooks the relative seclusion of the entrance courtyard.

On the ocean side the house is permeable and transparent, making the most of the stunning views

Inside are intimate family rooms and more transparent, open social areas, linked by a stairwell enclosed in translucent glass.

BELOW **Poised above the ocean, the house is like a ship in full sail.**
RIGHT, INSET **Entry is through a secluded courtyard.**
FAR RIGHT, INSET **The street side, intended to screen off the constant traffic, both visually and acoustically, is hermetic and impassive, with limited glazing. Its character is reversed on the ocean side, which opens up to the stunning light and views.**

and light. Recalling the breezy promenade decks of ocean liners, a generous wooden deck overlooks the sea. A smaller terrace also wraps around the master bedrooms above. The nautical allusions are emphasized in the sleek horizontality of the glass skin and the white wall planes.

Full-height glass walls slide back to connect the living areas with the external terraces, effortlessly dissolving space, while the changing play of light constantly animates the interior. A crisply detailed overhanging roof protects large areas of glass against potential overheating. The stairwell is enclosed by large panels of translucent glass, which filter and diffuse light into the space.

In spite of the urban density of the site, the courtyard typology and the flexibility of the sliding glass walls allow for different sorts of arrangements. The house is capable of accommodating one person or many with equal comfort. Connection to place is expressed by the urban character on the highway, by the marine spirit of the open terraces and decks, and by the varied relationships with carefully framed light and views.

The drama of the site demanded a strong response, and the architects proved more than capable of providing it. Floating above the beach and surf, this magical, light-filled eyrie is an idyllic retreat from the cares and bustle of modern California life.

ABOVE AND RIGHT **The breezy terraces and a glazed bedroom eyrie overlook the creamy California surf.**
OPPOSITE, MAIN PICTURE **Embodying a vigorous architectural response to the drama of the site, the house offers a civilized refuge from which to contemplate nature.**
OPPOSITE, ABOVE LEFT **Overhanging roofs resembling hat brims give shade to the large areas of glass.**
OPPOSITE, ABOVE RIGHT **Stunning ocean panoramas are reflected in the transparent skin.**
OPPOSITE, INSET **Sliding glazed walls separate the living space from the terraces, where the family can sunbathe and eat al fresco.**

Dominating the shoreline with its glass walls and long decks, the house is a modern manifestation of the California idyll of sun, sea, sand, and surf.

Rambling forest homestead

ARCHITECT: **MACK SCOGIN MERRILL ELAM**

It is still part of the great American dream to own a single family house on its own defined plot of land. Such a dwelling serves as a moated castle and refuge, a place in which to withdraw from the world, while house ownership is an emblem of worldly success.

For many Americans, their dream home is set in the suburbs and is likely to conform to one of two predominant styles: Colonial in the east and California ranch in the west. In a small number of cases, however, the house is transformed into a vehicle for personal expression for both client and architect. Despite changes in family structure, leisure time, and household technology, the basic house design brief remains essentially unchanged; yet, precisely because it is so thoroughly known, architects are at liberty to experiment and exercise their creativity. The house is also perhaps the only building type over which an architect can have complete design control and which allows him to establish a truly intimate client relationship, free of the often inhibiting influence of developers, cost managers, and bureaucrats. The house, then, is the repository of dreams and fantasies of both designer and occupant. In a nation that prizes originality and values individual expression, its cultural importance cannot be overstated.

This house in Maine, on the extreme reaches of the East Coast, was a wonderfully permissive commission that gave architects Mack Scogin Merrill Elam the freedom to explore and express an artistic agenda. Its owner, a painter and interior designer, moved from

LEFT **The house is a modern reinterpretation of the traditional Maine farmhouse typology, in which an accretion of elements creates a cluster of forms. A cubic tower marks the threshold and serves as the pivotal point of the plan.**
LEFT, INSET **The crisply orthogonal geometry of the tower makes a strong contrast with the lushness and wildness of nature.**
RIGHT **A ramp resembling a drawbridge leads up to the main entrance, providing a ceremonial approach.**

Held on slim columns, the house weaves through the forest and wraps around nature, bringing it into the heart of the dwelling.

OPPOSITE **The sharply angled living-room wing thrusts dramatically into the forest. The house is not an object building, but a complex configuration of linked volumes in close touch with nature. Porches offer vantage points from which to enjoy the magnificent surroundings.**
ABOVE **A rustic collage of materials evokes the textures and colors of the landscape.**
ABOVE RIGHT **In response to the sloping site, parts of the building are supported on slender, stiltlike columns that emulate the surrounding tree trunks and minimize footings on the ground, so the house disturbs the site as little as possible.**
RIGHT **The aperture in the wall enclosing the covered porch was designed to break down barriers with nature by allowing snow, rain, and light to enter the house.**
BELOW RIGHT **A long bench runs along the edge of the living room porch.**

Venice Beach in Los Angeles to Maine after the earthquake of 1994. She bought a plot in the White Mountains National Park overlooking a lake, where she commissioned the architects to design a two-bedroom house with ample space for living, painting, and entertaining. The brief included a request for distinct rooms, as opposed to more open, loftlike spaces, and a desire to be close to nature.

The site, which covers not much more than 2.5 acres, yields an intimate view across the lake to Lord's Hill, the easternmost boundary of the National Park. The hill, an inclined plane approaching the vertical, comforts with summer and spring greenery, dazzles with autumn colors, and shimmers and glistens in winter snow and ice.

For the architects, the site was the generator. Covered in a delicate carpet of mossy plants, it formed an extraordinarily fragile and beautiful ecosystem. Mack Scogin Merrill Elam's first design decision was that this should be disturbed as little as possible, so any new construction had to touch the ground lightly. The north side of the plot slopes up to a street; the south, down to a lake. A low concrete curb was used to divide the site into two parts, making a clear distinction between the man- and nature-oriented precincts.

The house is not a classic villa in a landscape. Rather, it is a clustered configuration of linked volumes and internal and external spaces. The overall arrangement is inspired by the traditional Maine farmstead, described by Merrill Elam as "big house, little house, back house, and barn. The front door is formal, but everything else is tagged on." This way of grouping rooms together in an extended cluster meant farmers could do their winter chores without being exposed to the harsh Maine climate. The architects also observed that the farmsteads usually

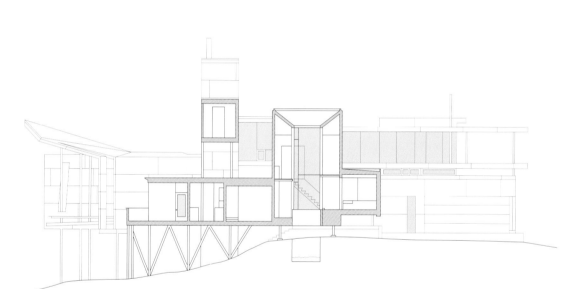

ABOVE LEFT **Stairs lead to the upper levels of the house; the way is marked by glimpses of the forest through vertical slashes of glazing.**
ABOVE CENTER **A spinal corridor links the front and rear of the house, threading together the various spaces.**
ABOVE **Wherever you are in the house, nature is never far away.**
LEFT **A cross-section through the stairwell and library shows that the house sits on an artificial extension of the ground plane, in response to the sloping site.**

Linking the floors in the center of the house is a glazed stairwell that provides room for a library.

OPPOSITE TOP LEFT **Taut sheets of steel form geometric balustrades connected to skinny tubular handrails. The integration of industrially made components contrasts with the surrounding landscape.**
OPPOSITE TOP RIGHT **On the upper level of the library stairwell is an intimate book-lined enclave.**
OPPOSITE BOTTOM LEFT **Glazing around the stairwell courtyard offers views through to other parts of the house.**
OPPOSITE BOTTOM RIGHT **The main staircase winds around a glazed two-story external void. Exposed to the elements, it conveys daylight into the deep recesses of the house.**

sat on a flat plane, unlike this site, so a new ground plane was built for the house, taking off from the saddle of the hill and moving out toward the pond, establishing a datum for the building.

The elements to the north of the dividing curb—the garage and zinc-sided painting studio—sit directly on the ground. South of the curb, the architects maximize views by lifting the house into the trees on wood and steel pilotis, or slender, stiltlike columns. The elevated floor plane reveals the rocky terrain that was embellished by Boston-based landscape architect Michael Van Valkenburgh with native plants. A switchback path crosses the site under the belly of the house, working its way toward the lake edge. Cement-board panels are bolted to the house's exterior walls and raised underbelly; the variegated light-gray siding responds to the effects of rain, snow, and sun with subtly expressive patterns.

A cubic tower marks the entrance and serves as the fulcrum of the pinwheel-shaped plan. Throughout the site, views are stunning, so there was no reason to privilege one direction over another. The tall, cement-board form encloses a stairwell leading into a long, stepped corridor. This spinal device links a set of small rooms that look and feel like elevated garden pavilions floating among the branches. The brief called for cellular rooms, opened up in various positions on the site to seem much bigger than they actually are, each with its own orientation. To the south and west, wings define and lock outdoor spaces into the plan. Thus the external, in-between spaces become a dynamic part of the house.

The house's constituent parts are disarmingly conventional, consisting of living and dining rooms, a kitchen, two bedrooms, and two screened sleeping porches. There is also a library, a drawing studio, a

detached painting studio and garage, and a small room for the owner's two dogs. Each room forms its own environment, through its separation from other spaces, and specific architectural responses to view, exposure, and function: choice of glass, placement of windows, shape of enclosing walls. Long corridors string the rooms loosely together, providing a visual and spacial harmony. This typology of an informal, tentacular plan form elevated above the ground extends the ideas behind the Chmar House in Atlanta, which Mack Scogin Merrill Elam Architects designed in 1990 and which led to this commission.

Although each room is roughly the same size, no one space is favored over another. The main bedroom includes an elaborate fireplace, even though the room is compact, and it differs radically from the guestroom, which opens onto a generous terrace with a cantilevered *brise-soleil* parapet. The hallways have extensive window walls, bringing light into the

Rooms are treated as distinct spaces, each distinguished by its place in the landscape, the shape of its enclosing walls, and the play of light.

interior. Lined with books, the main staircase winds around a mysterious glazed impluvium (from the Latin term for "rain"), a two-story external void exposed to the elements and another means of conveying light into the recesses of the house. Rainwater replenishes a pool in the center of the void. Reflections of books and sky mingle and play off the water, glass, and bookshelves. The material simplicity of the house is complemented with a few pieces of classic Modernist furniture, such as a Scandinavian dining table, and understated heirlooms. The architecture is allowed to speak, without being engulfed by clutter.

In their recent commissions, Mack Scogin Merrill Elam have explored riotous free-form geometries, but in this house there are relatively few exotic deviations. Only the living room breaks ranks from the orthogonal, opening up to vistas of the lake and mountains. Exterior walls slice outward to form a terrace, and one wall leans outwards, with a long hole punched through its thickness. The gesture is another way of connecting the house with nature; and the hole allows yet more light to permeate through the house.

Remarkably, the house manages to be both mature and enthusiastic: wise and disciplined, yet free and enchanting. Mack Scogin Merrill Elam may have abandoned Modernist notions of logic and order in their ingenious formal maneuvers throughout the house, but these moves are never gratuitous or narcissistic. They reveal a view, perform a particular function, or create a poetic pause in space and time. All this enriches the experience of being there.

Each constituent part of the plan is expressed volumetrically, within the external massing of the building, generating a complex, interlinked, abstract form, which seems to be in a constant state of movement against the backdrop of forest and mountain. In terms of experiencing space, the house appears to look back on itself, so you are never alone and always aware of other spaces, other views, and the presence of nature. The pinwheel-shaped plan creates a series of vantage points articulated as porches from which to savor the surroundings, and embraces an open area at the center of the site.

The use of slender pilotis to elevate parts of the house recalls Le Corbusier's Villa Savoye, an iconic Modernist house in its own grounds near Paris and, in many ways, the model for the modern villa. The Villa Savoye was also raised up on columns, allowing it to contemplate nature from a lofty height. Critical comparisons have been made between the two dwellings, but they are very different. The Villa Savoye is a compactly planned object building in the landscape, yet at the same time removed from it, suggesting permanence and solidity. By contrast, the rambling form of this Maine house, with its slim pilotis emulating the surrounding tree trunks, weaves and dodges through the forest like an informal encampment, becoming part of the landscape. Yet, although the house rests on the notion of the rural retreat, it also demonstrates an awareness of the continuing depth of primal human fear when brought face to face with nature and solitude.

Like a modern version of a tree house, the living room is a glazed eyrie hovering above the forest. Exterior walls skew outward, and one plane tilts in an almost ecstatic gesture to nature, with a long hole punched through its thickness. This part of the house is a vivid expression of the architects' predilection for riotous geometry. Angular and dramatic, the living room forms the prow of the house, a place of light, warmth, and shelter.

Glass plays a key role in opening up the house to spectacular views and light, emphasizing the strong connection with nature.

Interiors are carefully planned to reveal a view, filter light, or create a poetic pause, all of which contrive to enrich the spatial experience.

ABOVE **A modern hearth forms the focus of the living space, but instead of being solid and massive, it is set in a glazed wall, framed by trees, recreating the idea of a campfire in a forest.**
BELOW **A long, low window seat allows maximum enjoyment of the views.**
BELOW RIGHT **A view of the bathroom shows strips of glazing at high level.**
OPPOSITE **The prow of the living room launches boldly into the forest.**

Mack Scogin Merrill Elam have opened up the house so it looks inward as well as out to views. Never complete in its form, it reaches out to nature without trying to contain it in a closed courtyard. The architects reacted to the site, but also devised a house that could act as a companion to a single person. The house is deliberately configured so the owner can see the bedroom from the living room, for example, and light from other parts of the dwelling. The rooms are always in communication with each other.

Poignantly, the house marks a return to the forest and a return to the studio for an artist too long removed from both. The house breathes in the site, transfiguring it through a series of internal spatial events—framing, focusing, extending, enclosing, dismissing, and celebrating. Like Maine dwellings through history, this house is the result of form added on form, spaces adjoining defensively or closely clustering, resisting the long, harsh Maine winters and giving the impression of small "house towns."

Glass plays its part in the opening up of the house to light and views. Both clear and translucent glass are employed to create different levels of light transmission. While clear glass is extensively used in the walls of some rooms, framing and defining views, translucent glazing on the eastern wall, which overlooks the entrance, gently and subtly diffuses natural light, like a Japanese rice-paper screen. Other materials include a mixture of cement-board panels, zinc siding, concrete floors, and a wood-and-steel structural frame. Different textures and colors generate a rustic, collagelike effect, constantly surprising and delighting.

Movement through the house is rewarded by shifting views in an interior realm that favors no single viewpoint. A panoply of phenomena invites promenades of discovery—light and shade, for instance, are played out dramatically against an almost photographic black-and-white palette. The house is a reinterpretation the Modernist tradition of a villa elevated on pilotis into a new and highly poetic typology. Yet, despite its formal and material intricacy, the house feels simple and unforced. At the core of the architecture is a person and the design directly reflects an individual's needs and tastes. As Merrill Elam affectionately observes, "The house could not have been built for anyone else."

Return to the classic glass box

ARCHITECT: **TOM JESTICO AND VIVIEN FOWLER**

Cool and exquisitely minimal, the Miesian glass house is a potent archetype that continues to fascinate and inspire architects. Its attraction lies in its utter simplicity of form and flexible internal space, but it also requires a particular kind of site. Set in a beautiful walled garden, Tom Jestico and Vivien Fowler's house combines the openness of the classic Modernist box with tranquil seclusion. Yet they felt that Mies was too rigorous for their needs, and inspiration came as much from Charles and Ray Eames's house, which had much impressed Jestico when he visited it in the 1970s.

The site, in a rural corner of London, is typically suburban and unexceptional. Both the new house and its grounds are concealed within the confines of an old vegetable garden. Almost square in plan and bounded by 9ft-high brick walls, the ½ acre site is lush and fertile; it once produced fruit and vegetables for a health-food restaurant. When the owners acquired it, after years of neglect, it was overgrown and harbored a profusion of birds and butterflies, exuding a spellbinding charm. They were seduced.

The site forms part of a conservation area and, apart from greenhouses and sheds, had never been built on. Set back from the entrance, the new house is fronted by an expanse of west-facing lawn, which acts as an outdoor room. The boundary of the living space is therefore defined by the solid garden wall, rather than by the physical limits of the house itself. The relationship between the house and site is strong and simple: all the house can be seen from the garden and all the garden can be seen from the house. The success of the house as a flowing, uninhibited space hinges upon the impenetrability of the garden wall, which engenders a sense of privacy from within and of discretion from the outside.

The sequence of arrival and entry is carefully orchestrated. The only hint of the modern dwelling

Set in a beautiful walled garden, The house is a subtle and modern reinterpretation of the classic Miesian glass box. A fully glazed, steel-framed envelope forms a minimal barrier between the light-filled interior and the mature landscape. Simple glass panes and minimal glazing bars achieve a seamless effect. A wooden deck mediates between architecture and nature, and a cantilevered canopy gives protection from heat and glare.

Landscape plays an important part, with the replanted former vegetable garden forming an outdoor room around the house.

Crystalline and ethereal, the house is a transparent box hovering in its secret garden. The simple yet elegant modular structure forms a counterpoint to the richness and variety of the surrounding planting. Insulating blinds screen the perimeter when required. A boardwalk of varying widths surrounds the house, connected to the garden by a bridge crossing two ponds. The sleek and restrained glass pavilion is the antithesis of the family's former home, a four-story Victorian house.

TOP **The entrance leads to the storage and utility rooms at the heart of the house, around which are wrapped the living and dining spaces.**
ABOVE **There is an explicit visual connection between the dining space and the garden.**

OPPOSITE **The simple form of a steel frame infilled with glass allowed for rapid construction because no complex and messy wet trades were involved. In fact, the house was completed by the family in the evenings and at weekends.**

beyond is an entryphone set in the old brickwork. Visitors enter through a small door punched into the perimeter wall. (There is also a larger double gate for car access.) Crossing over this threshold into the secret garden, the house appears as an ethereal glass pavilion floating in its luxuriant grounds. Topped by a crisp, flat roof, the single-story house is of relatively modest proportions. A boardwalk of varying width surrounds the glass box, connected to the garden by what appears to be a bridge crossing two ponds. (The bridge is, in fact, a cellar converted from an old engine house.)

The owners wanted the house to be as open as possible, but also robust enough to accommodate their family comfortably. They were also determined that the design should be uncompromisingly modern, avoiding the cumbersome compartmentalization often found in English houses. The solution is both elegant and economical, taking the form of a fully glazed, steel-framed envelope flanked by a wooden deck that mediates between the transparent interior and the verdant landscape. Elevations are composed of simple glass panes defined with minimal glazing bars to achieve a seamless effect. To limit heat loss, the double-glazed skin has a low-emissivity coating. Overhanging louvered screens also protect the glass

walls from glare and the buildup of heat. Tom Jestico describes the plan as resembling a 1960s office building, with an enclosed node of services surrounded by open space. The compact form results in an economic floor-to-wall ratio, which reduces siding costs and offsets heat losses. The house is based on a 13 x 13 ft structural bay with a 9ft ceiling height. Two internal bays house a central core of serviced spaces such as utility rooms and linking corridor. The five-column structure creates a strong geometry, rhythmically articulating the elevations.

Within the symmetrical and regular structural form lies an asymmetrical and informal living space that wraps fluidly around the central core and overlooks the garden. To the rear, order is restored, with three cellular bedrooms and a study following the lines of the structural grid. Despite the simple modular structure, the internal spaces have great subtlety and refinement, derived from thoughtful inflection and articulation of spaces and elements. Finishes are understated yet elegant: maple strip flooring, white walls, frosted-glass doors, and granite counters.

The landscape forms an integral part of the overall project. Because the site was cleared prior to the house's construction, the garden is new,

OPPOSITE **The sense of a series of flowing, uninhibited spaces hinges upon the impenetrability of the garden wall, which creates a formal boundary, engendering a strong sense privacy from within.**
TOP AND ABOVE LEFT **The surrounding boardwalk terrace is integrated with the house so seamlessly that the master bedroom seems almost to be part of the garden.**
ABOVE CENTER **Finishes are understated yet elegant, adding to the thoughtful sum of parts.**
ABOVE RIGHT **Lightweight partitions are used to enclose and define space.**

with only a handful of original elements remaining—notably, some low boxtree hedges, fruit trees and firs. A new lawn has been laid, and quick-growing silver birches, native to local heathland, have been planted around the perimeter.

In practical terms, the house was put together with great ease and speed. The project was managed by its architect owners using directly appointed trade contractors, and the house was built by the family in their spare time. Throughout, from the overall design concept down to the smallest details, Jestico sought to achieve delight through simplicity. Appropriate for its setting, the house reconciles style and economy with a light touch. You sense that even Mies van der Rohe, godfather of the glass box, would have approved.

Light-filled internal spaces gain a sense of sober refinement from a carefully chosen palette of understated materials combined with contemporary furniture.

LEFT **The house is so well integrated with the landscape that its overall scale is hard to grasp. From some approaches, the building seems to merge with its thickly wooded setting, while from other directions, it has a solid, intimidating presence.**
BELOW, LEFT TO RIGHT
Concrete planes and wooden decks shape external rooms that extend beyond the living area into the landscape. A right-angled concrete wall reaches out beyond the western end of the house. Wood-framed glass walls give the interior a lightness and transparency, dissolving the building's volume and making a connection with nature in all its wild magnificence.
RIGHT **The austerity of the concrete planes is tempered and softened by planting.**

Sheer mountain house

ARCHITECT: **MACK SCOGIN MERRILL ELAM**

One of the threads running through American architecture, and American Modernism in particular, is the relationship of building to landscape. The idea of blending in and blurring the distinctions between inside and out is identified especially with Frank Lloyd Wright's organically inspired Prairie houses. By contrast, the notion of defining a formal, almost urban realm within the wilderness of nature informs such memorable architectural set pieces as Thomas Jefferson's University of Virginia campus, completed in the early 19th century.

These two models coexist in the design of a house in the Appalachian foothills of Georgia by Atlanta-based architects Mack Scogin Merrill Elam. The strategy of working with the grain of the land, embodied in a long, low plan spread over a single story, has clear overtones of Frank Lloyd Wright's work. More pragmatically, it will also enable its clients to use it not only as a weekend retreat, but also

as their main home after retirement. While some contemporary architecture glorifies the collision of building elements or forces, this Mountain House seeks a sense of balance and equilibrium. Designed for a couple with varied backgrounds and interests, the house accommodates differences by finding common ground. The outcome is a dwelling that is both urban and rural, formal and informal, casual and deliberate, but never contradictory.

The clients, whose children by previous marriages are grown up and now live elsewhere, have their roots in different parts of America and pursue separate careers: he is a journalist and avid collector of regional art; she is a gardener and landscape designer. But, just as they have learned to share in each other's professional lives, the house also brings contrasting elements together: inside and out, solid and void,

light and shade, intimacy and openness. The first clue to the delicate balancing act achieved by Mack Scogin Merrill Elam is the entrance court, a sweeping drive rustically paved with local stone, around which the main parts of the house are clustered. The architects relished the idea of placing this urban element in a rural setting, in the manner of French and English country estates. The juxtaposition of city and country is heightened by the centrally placed screened porch on the entrance court that offers carefully framed vistas through the porch toward the trees, before you have even left your car. The house grows increasingly informal as visitors move to and through it. Placed at one corner of the court, the main entrance leads to a double-height gallery filled with the couple's evocative and colorful collection of regional art. From this tall but constricted space, you pass into the generous, open living

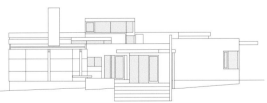

ABOVE **The guest suite overlooks a lawn and pond. Shown below it are the house's south and east elevations.**
FAR LEFT, TOP TO BOTTOM **Harmony between house and setting is evident in the play of reflections on glass, the bold artwork in the hall, the layout of the entrance court, and the detail of a corner window.**

room with its sweeping views down the hillside to a grassy pasture and the mountains beyond. Here the transition from city to countryside is complete.

The large volume of the property is broken down into three major elements—the main house, a guest house and garage, and the screened porch—yet its overall scale remains enigmatic. Depending on how you approach the building, it creates intriguing illusions of size. From some perspectives, it seems

to merge with and disappear into the landscape, while from another approach its cantilevered roofs, like broad hat brims, endow it with a powerful presence.

Set in the foothills of the Appalachian Mountains less than 1 mile (1.5km) from Georgia's border with North Carolina, the secluded site is thickly wooded and surrounded by rolling mountains. With its long, low volumes and strong horizontal emphasis, the house hugs the ground, forming a deliberate contrast

Although the land was heavily wooded when the present owners acquired it, it had been cleared and farmed earlier in the 20th century.

with the verticality of the hills and the slender birches and poplars. A small stream runs across its southern edge, supplying power for an old grist mill and water for horses in a neighbor's pasture. Drawn by the landscape, light, and tranquility, an artists' colony has been established nearby.

While the site is undeniably beautiful, it presented a number of challenges. The initial one was finding the most suitable place to build. An old farmhouse had once stood at the foot of a large oak tree near the road leading to the site, and the clients originally hoped to build there. But, after walking around with with the architects and builder, they concluded that the house should sit further in on flatter land that had more privacy and offered better views of the pasture. This meant constructing a long driveway, but the builder found evidence of an old existing access road and used it as the outline for the new drive, adjusting the route to preserve as many trees as possible. The base of the drive was used to form a dam and create

a pond west of the new house. Another potentially problematic site condition was an abundance of water. The local climate is extremely damp—indeed, this part of Georgia is of one the wettest places on the eastern seaboard of the U.S. To counteract the effects of the wet weather, concrete footings and foundations were built to create a partial basement, allowing water to run around the house and down the stream to the south. However, it was discovered that many local subcontractors were capable of executing high-quality concrete work, as a result of the need for retaining walls in a hilly, wet landscape, so concrete as well as glass developed into a key element in the design.

Concrete is used for both practical and expressive purposes. Forming the foundations and base of the house, it performs much of the heavy structural work, but it is also used to extend the house into the landscape, forging a link between ground and architecture. An exposed concrete wall running

through the kitchen and entrance gallery, and a concrete chimney, help to anchor the house to the land. At the same time, a right-angled concrete wall reaches out beyond the western end of the house, partially enclosing an outdoor room. On the opposite side, another concrete wall extends past the guest house. The solidity of the concrete is tempered by the lightness and transparency of the wooden-framed glass walls, which dematerialize the architecture so the roof planes appear to be simply hovering in midair, with no visible means of support. The slender wood frames echo the slim trunks of the surrounding birches.

Although largely wood-framed, the house has some steel elements. The screened porch is framed in steel, and steel beams were used in some of the cantilevered roofs. The longest cantilever, however, is supported by wooden trusses that, because they run deep into the living room, can extend far beyond the building envelope without the aid of steel.

ABOVE LEFT **Elegant Modernist furniture and rugs complement the architecture in the spacious living room, which is linked to external terrace decks by sliding doors. The room is suffused with a delicate, shimmering light. Clerestory windows capture and diffuse radiance from above and give the impression that the roof is floating over the space. The owners love the changing quality of light that animates the space.**
ABOVE **Strips of glazing at the top and bottom of walls break up their mass.**
RIGHT, TOP TO BOTTOM **The main bedroom, on the northern side of the house, has low windows incised into the walls. It is linked to the kitchen and entrance hall by a long corridor, which provides space for displaying the owners' art collection. Bare concrete walls act as a neutral backdrop for vivid paintings.**
FAR LEFT **Windows have been placed to form abstract geometric patterns.**

ABOVE **Steps lead up to the raised terrace enclosing the living space. Sheer planes of glass separate the interior and the exterior.**
BELOW, LEFT TO RIGHT **The rustic yet elegant character of the living room is reinforced by polished wood floors. Plywood chairs based on a classic design by the architects Charles and Ray Eames evoke the spirit of functional Modernism. The sculptural forms of the chairs cast bulbous shadows on the wood floor.**

In terms of a brief, the clients asked for just two things: wall space for their artworks and extensive views out to the landscape. As part of the balancing act that characterizes the project, the architects opened up the house along much of its southern side, with vistas to the creek and pasture. A long porch also emphasizes the connection with the exterior. The northern side is more closed off, providing the wall space necessary to display the clients' art collection.

Although the sweep of the interior is predominantly horizontal, vertical accents are provided in places such as the entrance gallery and part of the master bedroom. Interiors are suffused with a shimmering light, both from the sun and the moon. The clients were struck by the way the light animates the whole house. They also like the fact that the screened porch acts as a second living room, playing country cousin to the more urban indoor one on the opposite side. Equipped with a built-in concrete bench, together with a large grill hanging from a central chimney, and radiant heating in the concrete floor, the porch can be used all year round for entertaining. These expansive, semipublic spaces can easily accommodate a crowd, yet hideaways are scattered through the house, such as the inglenook behind the living-room

fireplace, the study tucked inside the entrance gallery, and a little bay window on the master bathroom that opens out on a private court enclosed by hemlocks. By setting the guest house just a few steps away from the main house, a sense of privacy is achieved while maintaining the feeling of a closely knit compound. Although small, the guest house is a comfortable, self-contained refuge with its own outdoor porch overlooking one of the site's two ponds.

The house embodies some admittedly radical moves, such as focusing the plan on the void of a screened porch and treating the entrance court as a raised plateau; yet ultimately they do not seem out of place. These details, together with the use of clerestory windows to illuminate the interior and the house's exaggerated horizontal lines, strongly recall the work of Wright and reinforce a wider connection with American Modernism. Such affinities are more in the nature of family resemblances, however, inflected by context and brief, than simply direct quotations. At once part of the surrounding forest, yet cutting through it to frame views and enclose outdoor spaces, the Mountain House is a celebration of a finely judged symbiosis between architecture and nature.

ABOVE **A freestanding fireplace backed by an intimate inglenook is the focal point of the living room, where the abundance of clerestory windows strongly recalls the work of Frank Lloyd Wright and reinforces a wider connection with American Modernism. In common with many of Wright's buildings, the house reflects a finely judged balance between architecture and nature.**

Intimate nooks and alcoves add a human aspect to the dynamic spatial drama of the living room.

MAIN PICTURE **A sweeping approach to the house culminates in an entrance courtyard paved with local stone. The architects relished the idea of placing the courtyard, an essentially urban element, in a rural setting.** INSET **Compared with the openness of the southern side of the house, the northern side is more closed off to the outside world, but its interior wall offers plenty of space for hanging pictures.**

Throughout the 20th century—and on into the 21st—the notions of lightness and transparency have exerted a particularly seductive and tenacious hold on the architectural imagination. Although glass is a familiar substance, modern manufacturing processes have transformed it into one of the most valuable and versatile materials of the present day. With this evolution, new conceptual languages in architecture have become possible. These are still being developed and explored, from the simple provision of light and views without loss of warmth, to the creation of masterpieces. The notion of the modern glass house as a pavilion set in splendid isolation in luxuriant landscape is still a seductive one, but in cities and urban areas, the conception of a glass house takes on a very different edge. Here there is equal scope for invention and ingenuity, taking advantage of height and views and working with existing buildings. Such challenges give rise to new approaches, whether it is opening up a high-rise apartment through the use of glass or building from scratch on an urban site, framing and defining views and privacy by means of transparent or translucent screens. Glass architecture, once deemed purely utopian, is now a remarkable reality.

Floor-to-ceiling windows minimize the visual barriers to the setting. The delicacy and ethereal qualities of glass are exploited to create a striking contrast between the intimacy of the living area and the panoramic splendor of Los Angeles lying below.

A loft in Milan

ARCHITECT: **RODOLFO DORDONI**

OPPOSITE **A double-height living space forms the focus of the house. Windows are punched into the concrete shell, bringing light into the tall, luminous interior. The large panes of glass are held in slim aluminum frames.**
ABOVE **A dining table with Eames chairs reflects the elegant yet functional spirit of Dordoni's conversion. The building originally formed part of an industrial complex on the edge of Milan. Other buildings on the site have also been appropriated and remodeled for other uses.**
RIGHT, ABOVE RIGHT, AND BELOW **The living space looks out on a garden and pool. Thick red curtains form a striking flash of color in the predominantly white interior.**

This transformation of a former industrial building into a living and work space in Milan is part of a now familiar 20th-century urban phenomenon. As old factories and workshops become obsolete, they are colonized and converted to new uses rather than lying abandoned. This pattern of development has its origins in the loft movements of 1950s and 1960s New York.

The original lofts were basic shells, often without proper sanitation or heating, but they had the luxury of space and light from high ceilings and tall windows. Most were found in cast-iron-framed warehouses designed in the 19th century to house light industrial manufacturing processes. Despite their apparently mundane function, they were innovative structures. The method of cast-iron-frame construction was devised to create buildings of multiple storys with large open-plan floors, ideal for manufacturing or industrial activities. The use of cast-iron frames also began to free the facade from its traditional load-bearing function and allow large expanses of glass to fill entire spaces between columns. Social and economic changes resulted in the abandonment of such large, flexible buildings, and as a result, landlords were eager to entice new tenants.

The loft pioneers were artists and bohemians, taking advantage of affordable space. Cannibalizing old warehouses provided units that were cheap enough to rent and sizeable enough in which to live and work. This home-cum-studio is the origin of the modern loft, but precedents for the open-plan loft living space can also be discerned in the ideals of Modernism and in the purpose-built artists' ateliers

Imaginative and sensitive remodeling has breathed new life into a redundant industrial building.

of the very early 20th century. From their gritty origins in the 1950s, lofts have become one of the most diverse international building types. Developers in almost every city with a stock of run-down industrial buildings have begun converting them and selling space as shell units. Loft culture is still evolving, and reaching cities as geographically distant as Helsinki and São Paulo. In the 1970s, the concept of adaptive re-use grew into an architectural discipline, particularly in North America. In this respect, lofts became an important part of strategies for urban renewal. Building on the American experience, the notion of turning redundant industrial sites into places for living gradually took hold in Europe.

The openness of the loft interior presents a reassuring honest visibility. Glass walls are commonly used both on the external facades and internally to delineate living spaces yet maintain a sense of transparency. To some extent, the original ideal of loft living—maximum space at minimum cost—has been compromised by developers in recent years. Now loft living has become another real-estate cliché, and sleekly styled warehouse conversions in desirable inner-city areas change hands for huge sums—a far cry from the American artist Robert Rauschenberg's experience in the early 1950s of living in downtown Manhattan for $10 a month. Yet the principle of having the freedom to make your home whatever you want it to be still makes the concept highly seductive.

In Italy, a country rich in historic architecture, the renovation of more recent industrial structures has been slower to catch on than in New York or London.

FAR LEFT **White walls and concrete floors form an austere backdrop to furniture and art objects. The interior is flooded with light from the tall windows.**
FAR LEFT, INSET **A studio space overlooks the living room on the upper level.**
LEFT **A staircase separates the large open-plan volume from cellular rooms.**
THIS PICTURE **The interior has an imposing scale. A purpose-designed aluminum table with slim legs runs along the edge of the studio mezzanine, acting as a balustrade.**

There are simply too many older and more precious historical relics demanding attention; consequently, industrial buildings seldom figure in the scheme of preservation priorities. The loft is still a relative rarity in Milan, because of the lack of large open-plan spaces in the city's center. However, there is no shortage of factories and warehouses on the periphery, and gradually these are being appropriated for new uses.

Rodolfo Dordoni's transformation of a redundant building in Milan's industrial hinterland celebrates the gutsy character of the original architecture, but it also has certain characteristics that clearly distinguish it from the conventional New York loft space. First, it is freestanding, like a family house, as opposed to being part of a larger warehouse or factory. It also overlooks a garden, thereby establishing a connection with the exterior. Originally a cafeteria and locker room in an old industrial complex southwest of Milan, the building fell into disuse when industry moved away. Nearly all the old warehouses and workshops in the district have been converted into dwellings, offices, and studios, becoming splendid open-plan spaces that combine the gritty character of industrial architecture with the panache of Italian design.

Set in its own grounds, Dordoni's building is a simple, two-story rectangular block made largely of concrete. His conversion strives to maximize space and light by punching large glazed openings into the concrete shell. A powerful contrast is engendered between the massive concrete walls and the new windows with their sheer panes of glass held in slim aluminum frames.

The double-height living area overlooks a garden, and a square swimming pool set against the side of the house adds to the hedonistic air. A strip of cellular rooms containing a guest bedroom, laundry, and kitchen is arranged along the long edge of the living space. The kitchen connects with the dining

Materials and furnishings that reflect a refined modern spirit complement the simplicity of the interior. The effect is understated yet elegant.

room, which in turn melds fluidly into the living area. Running lengthwise across the plan, a narrow staircase separates the main living area from the smaller rooms. This leads to the upper floor, which is more private and sequestered, but also has its moments of drama. A mezzanine work studio overlooks the living area, taking advantage of views and light, and enhancing the sense of encounter between the two levels.

On each side of the studio is a bedroom with its own connecting bathroom. The bathroom of the master bedroom is particularly spacious, a true

ABOVE **The kitchen overlooks an enclosed courtyard lushly planted to create a screen of greenery. Tall glass walls admit light and strengthen links with the exterior. The project combines some of the best aspects of loft living with those of freestanding houses. The setting lets the occupants take advantage of being outside—a pleasure usually denied urban loft dwellers.**
RIGHT AND FAR RIGHT **Kitchen furniture and fixtures were specially designed by the architect. A mahogany table adjoins a marble-topped work unit. Stylish "Ant" chairs by Danish designer Fritz Hansen complete the picture. The functional spirit reflects the building's industrial origins.**

salle de bain, with a central tub and double sink with marble top. The sides of the bathtub are finished in smooth enameled plaster.

Unwinding with a fluid grace, the continuity of the various spaces is emphasized by a uniformity of materials. Raw concrete is used for the floors, polished and sealed so it gleams with a smooth luster. The staircase is covered in fir, providing an element of organic warmth against the sleek, hard concrete. Walls are uniformly covered in white plaster with a finish of white paint, enhancing the prevailing sense of lightness. In the bathrooms, shimmering gray glass mosaic tiles line the bathtubs. Light floods through the lofty interior, reflected off the plain white walls and glossy concrete floors.

This limited palette of materials forms a neutral backdrop to an array of carefully chosen furniture that reflects the elegant yet functional spirit of the best Modernist design. The mahogany table in the kitchen adjoins a cooking surface with a top made of delicately veined Carrara marble. Built into masonry

Isolated from the domestic milieu below, yet at the same time still part of it, the mezzanine studio overlooks the living space and enjoys wonderful light and views. The insertion of a mezzanine to provide an additional sleeping or working area has become a well-rehearsed architectural ploy in the conversion of industrial buildings, but in this case Rodolfo Dordoni gives it a contemporary and memorable twist. In a particularly ingenious use of space, a long work table acts as a balustrade.

THIS PICTURE **The bathroom, lined with shimmering gray glass mosaic tiles, is visible from the master bedroom. The bathroom has been conceived as a generously proportioned *salle de bain*, complete with a freestanding bathtub, which can just be seen on the left. Light filters into the space through a series of side windows.**

niches and arranged in islands, the kitchen fixtures were specially designed by Dordoni. Kitchen chairs are the famous "Ant" model by Danish designer Fritz Hansen. Around the dining table are distinctive plastic bucket armchairs, originally designed Charles and Ray Eames, mounted on spindly "Eiffel Tower" bases. The choice of materials and furnishings is intended to complement the austere simplicity of the interior and reflect its industrial origins.

This Milan loft also reflects the way in which such spaces have become a model for a creative way of life, where work and domestic activities are one. In that it represents both home and work, hedonism and domesticity, public and private space, loft living is paradoxical. In this case, the large neutral space is equally suitable for family life and for concentrated work. The upstairs mezzanine studio is isolated from the domestic milieu below, yet at the same time is still part of it, sharing the same light and views.

The insertion of a mezzanine either for sleeping or working is a well-rehearsed architectural move that originated in the storage mezzanines of warehouses, but also in artists' studios in turn-of-the-20th-century Paris. These light-filled, purpose-built apartments provided height for large canvases and a small mezzanine space for artists to sleep in. The form of this space has become associated with creative achievement and established a model, developed by Modernist architects, which is now a common and logical ploy in the subdivision of large volumes.

ABOVE **The main bedroom overlooks the garden. The dressing table is from the "Nomos" line by Norman Foster, continuing the theme of elegant, yet functional architect-designed furniture. A cluster of paintings adds color and spontaneity.**
TOP AND RIGHT **A long mirror in the master bathroom creates the illusion of more space and reflects light. For privacy, the windows are partly filled with translucent glass.**

On the upper level, bedrooms and bathrooms are intimate havens of light and colour, calculated to engage and stimulate the senses.

THIS PICTURE **A glazed door in the walled entrance courtyard offers a tantalizing glimpse of the delights within.** INSET **The main living space is enclosed by a huge glass roof.** ABOVE RIGHT, LEFT TO RIGHT **From the roof terrace, there are wide views over north London and down into the living room below. Translucent glass fins act as terrace screens.** FAR RIGHT **Light floods down through the roof to illuminate the double-height living room.**

Neomodern palazzo

ARCHITECT: **RICK MATHER**

The leafy, well-heeled enclaves of north London have long been the setting for some of the most intriguing and progressive experiments in domestic architecture. Maxwell Fry's Sun House of 1935 and Ernö Goldfinger's row of houses at Willow Road in Hampstead presaged the arrival of Modernism in a sceptical England. In particular, Fry's Sun House, with its dazzling, white-rendered walls, nautical balcony supported on slender steel columns, and large areas of glass, evoked a new era of open, airy, healthy living, worlds away from the dingy confines of traditional Victorian and Georgian houses that dominate the city. Built for enlightened and adventurous clients, such dwellings epitomized Le Corbusier's mantra of *soleil, espace, verdure* (sun, light, greenery) transplanted to the genteel confines of a suburban setting.

On an urban hilltop site, a house by Rick Mather could easily be mistaken for an early Modernist icon. Seen from the road, it gives little away, a modest mass set back a full house-width from the street, with inscrutable white walls rising from behind an enclosed entrance courtyard. In streets lined with solid, brown-brick villas, the Mediterranean whiteness of this upstart newcomer is slightly shocking. But there are many more delicious surprises within.

Mather is known for his ability to remix and energize Modernist ideas in a way that might be regarded with scepticism by die-hard academics and architectural theorists, but that tends to generate popular support for modern architecture. He also has an imaginative approach to materials, exploring new and different ways of using and combining them.

If you were to consider what might be an ideal commission for an architect like Mather, you would have to concede—despite his forays into other more utilitarian genres, such as student housing and speculative offices—that a new house for an impressively rich and enthusiastic client would spring to mind. The house is a luxurious mini-palazzo for an aspiring modern Medici. Here Mather has all the space and indulgence he needs to refine and intensify his neo-Modernist approach. His work is characterized by the fluid interpenetration of space, achieved by creating vertical, horizontal, and three-dimensional visual links between the various spaces and elements that reveal the building's wider

Vertical, horizontal, and three-dimensional visual elements create links between the airy spaces.

LEFT **Mather's innovative use of glass reinforces links with the outside, so that people indoors are always aware of constantly changing British weather conditions and the intensity of the light. In this area overlooking the garden, horizontal glass meets vertical in a seamless sweep. Glazed slits in the floor transmit light to the basement pool, giving glimpses of a mysterious subterranean realm.**
THIS PICTURE **An imposing, fluid volume drenched in light, the double-height living area is the nucleus of the house.**
FAR RIGHT, TOP **A walled terrace extends the living area. Protected by an external blind, the huge south-facing skylight recalls the large windows in artists' studios.**
FAR RIGHT, BOTTOM **The main staircase is made of clear glass. Its crystalline treads encourage light transmission.**

dimension and maximize the transmission of light. An intoxicating sense of spatial freedom within the confines of the building envelope is the hallmark of Mather's architecture, and this house has a multitude of such devices, and much more besides.

The client wanted a house that would go beyond mere convenience and become a work of art in its own right. Mather was selected out of five architects interviewed, and his sketch solution to a complex brief was accepted at once. The new house replaces an existing 1950s property and is a striking usurper amid its more staid neighbors. Light penetrates the basic block of the house's mass from all directions. A single huge lightwell pierces the heart of the building down to a pool at basement level. Light floods down through this void, unobstructed in its descent, since the main staircase is made of clear glass, its delicate treads sparkling and weaving through space. Other large volumes are carved out to form rooms, while a couple of planes splice through the building mass.

An electronically controlled gate provides a suitably Bondlike entry sequence. The house is dug into the sloping site, so from the street side it appears a modest two storys high. At the rear, however, it opens up to three storys overlooking a secluded garden. An entrance hall leads past the scintillating glass staircase to the main volume of the living and dining area, a dramatic double-height space topped by a glass roof. Light floods down through the roof, bathing the living area in light. The glass heightens the connection with the outside; occupants are aware of every nuance of weather and light.

Glazed slits in the floor give tantalizing glimpses into the watery realm below. (At times, when the floor appears to dissolve under your feet, the effect can be slightly alarming.) You can walk across the stairwell gallery into the living room and dining area,

Even on the darkest day, light floods down into the living area from a south-facing skylight.

partially divided by a glass section cut into the floor. This glass floor meets the western elevation in what appears to be a seamless expanse of transparency.

The living area forms the nucleus of the plan, with the kitchen placed on the street side overlooking a small vegetable garden. On the second floor, bedrooms and bathrooms are arranged in an L shape around the void of the living room. Balustrades around the void are made from thin planes of glass, minimally and seamlessly detailed, adding to the sense of lightness and lack of materiality. The sequence of sliding planes and floating volumes focuses attention on space itself. The arrangement of the spaces and their illumination is enhanced by the unexpected fluidity of the structure. In this way, the primacy of the structure is overcome by the power of the spaces

Astonishingly delicate
and crystalline, the
staircase appears to
hover lightly in space,
like a glass sculpture.

LEFT **The glass staircase
gives the impression that
it is suspended in a void.**
BELOW **From the entrance
hall, the living room
unfolds in a fluid sequence,
with views through to the
rear garden.**
RIGHT, TOP TO BOTTOM
**The use of glazing throughout
the house is beautifully and
enviably seamless.**

and the visual links between them. Architectural ideas are heightened, rather than being subject to the standard reading of the structure—just as abstraction in painting emphasizes ideas that might not be revealed in a conventional rendering.

This is Modernism in the best tradition, owing a debt to the classic villas of Le Corbusier. Although horizontal sheets of plate glass are used to enclose and screen the immediate pool environment, the space rises vertically from the lowest to the highest levels. The flow of space through all three storys creates a sense of sculptural intent. The main window—a south-facing skylight protected by an external blind—restates the historical link with the artists' studios of Paris that first incorporated big windows. Even on the dingiest day, the space is suffused with an extraordinary radiance. In brilliant sunshine, the effect is spectacular. The use of glass, whether horizontal or vertical, transparent or mirrored, creates a kind of blur, an uncertainty about limits that makes the interior very different from traditional historical models, with their clearly defined cellular rooms.

Attached to the study area, a small balcony looks back into the body of the house, providing a vantage point from which to savor the entire interior. From here, the composition opens up in all directions, anchored by a blank panel that screens the bedroom

corridor directly opposite. This is reminiscent of devices in Corbusier's early houses, in which a sculptural mass is used to stabilize spatial flow. But, unlike Corbusier, Mather introduces narrow slots of glazing to clarify and define massing. The composition is overlaid by the constant play of light, whether transmitted directly from the sky through the huge areas of glazing, or reflected upward from the pool.

Like transparent blades, the upper edges of the glass balustrades slice into the air, blurring contours with their reflections, while also defining them with

surgical precision. The glass treads treat circulation as a theatrical promenade, as opposed to a practical motion. Even without the sun's gleaming presence, the horizontal planes of glass and the pool reflect the diagonal form of the stairs, suggesting an Escherlike ambiguity and the desire to escape from gravity.

At the same time, the house is laid out with great practicality—for example, in placing the two single bedrooms/studies in the corners of the ground floor, making them suitable for guests or grandchildren. It is also sensitive to the outside prospect, so main windows are directed at the most idyllic views. In addition to molding dynamic internal space, the huge white walls screen the surrounding buildings, strategically isolating and emphasizing views. In this respect, the house is an object lesson in showing what can be lost by the "Miesian glass box" approach of opening up the elevations on all sides and how

The lower ground floor is given over to an enormous swimming pool—a sparkling lagoon of sensual pleasure.

much more convincing and reassuring it is to be able to filter out the exterior with solid walls as opposed to, for instance, flimsy Venetian blinds. On a final practical note, amply proportioned corridors and closets allow the swift and efficient transformation of domestic disarray into pristine orderliness.

The house has no covered garages, so front and rear gardens are conceived as a series of coherent spaces that extend the building's outer domain, with a paved herb garden on the public side and a classic tree-lined lawn to the rear. Generous provision is made for sitting-out areas next to all the major spaces, for enjoying in good weather. Full of light from all sides brought together in a complex and magical synthesis, the house epitomizes the rare quality of being both a marvelous place to live as well as an impressive and memorable piece of architecture.

Mather's work shows some affinities with the High Tech school, particularly in its lightness and

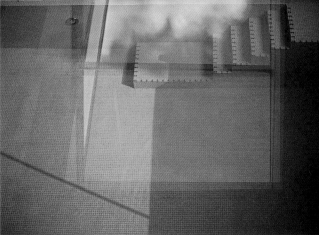

OPPOSITE **The pool that occupies the lower ground floor forms a magical cavern. The staircase is reflected in the glass and water.**
ABOVE RIGHT AND RIGHT **Light percolates through the staircase, casting dappled shadows, while gauzy reflections add to the air of languid sensuality.**
BELOW **Cross-sections show the arrangement of spaces and the central stairwell.**

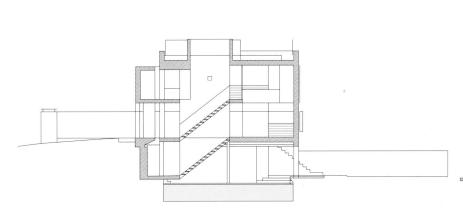

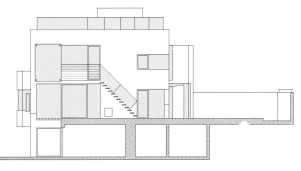

transparency and in its preference for hard, machine-worked materials, yet it does not lend itself to simple classification and always remains sensitive to context and the specifics of program. The notion of context is, first and foremost, the city, and in particular the residential London of Georgian rowhouses and their Victorian extensions. Yet it is obvious from Mather's London houses, of which this villa is a model example, that his concept of the city does not embrace the slavish imitation and reproduction of traditional forms. Rather, it suggests that the city is a organically evolving environment, in which contemporary buildings form part of a reciprocal dialogue. In terms of the physical character of his

Mather avoids fetishistic ornamentation, concentrating instead on the use of space, light, and exquisitely refined materials.

LEFT Enclosed by sliding glass
screens that can be pulled
back in warm weather, the
swimming pool is a luscious,
luminous, subterranean
space. Light is reflected
off the water and diffused
throughout the house.
THIS PICTURE The three-
story elevation overlooking
the garden is a taut geometric
exercise in white walls and
large planes of glass. In
its abstraction, purity, and
Mediterranean whiteness,
it evokes the optimistic age
of early English Modernism—
of which there are many
examples in this part of London.
BELOW A pebbled pool runs
along the outside edge of the
glass wall, connecting with
the swimming pool inside.

architecture, Mather clearly relishes using reflective
or transparent materials, particularly stainless steel
and glass in all its forms. This form of decoration has
a distant ancestor in Adolf Loos, the influential
Modernist pioneer, who exploited the sensuous
surface qualities of materials to create an effect of
luxury that was no longer dependent on handicraft.
Yet, balanced by a strong formal control—even a
certain minimalism—Mather's work avoids the trend
of fetishistic ornamentation, concentrating instead
on the essence of architecture: space, light, and
exquisitely refined materials.

Hollywood haven

ARCHITECT: **RICHARD NEUTRA/MARMOL RADZINER**

THIS PICTURE **The Lew House, built by Richard Neutra, benefits from a magnificently elevated vantage point, with the city of Los Angeles unfolding below.**
INSET **The two-story dwelling is entered from the upper floor at street level. Steps at the rear lead down to a sloping yard.**
RIGHT **The compact entrance hall has views through to the living space beyond.**

An Austrian émigré who settled in the U.S. in the early 1920s, Richard Neutra was a Modernist's Modernist. Neutra's architecture is a sophisticated equation, a methodology honed to respond to three variables: site, client, and budget. Throughout his career, which spanned over half a century from 1915 to the late 1960s, his domestic architecture was a methodical search for a flexible, organic armature for living, as opposed to a series of contrived, one-off solutions.

One of Neutra's earliest projects was the Lovell Health House, the first steel-framed house in the U.S., completed in 1929. The house lent itself easily to photography and secured Neutra his international reputation. Equally significantly, it was also a house that addressed the art of living in Los Angeles, a city of wide, flat valleys interrupted by canyons and hills.

THIS PICTURE **At the rear of the house, an external balcony and deck run alongside the long glazed volume of the living room. Sliding glass doors separate the deck from the interior, so in warm weather it becomes an extension of the living area. A characteristic of Neutra's houses is that the conventionally opaque boundary between indoors and out is replaced by a thin sheet of glass, minimizing the barrier between people and the natural world.**

INSET **The carport on the street side of the house doubles as an outdoor living area. Thin Venetian blinds screen it from the rest of the living area.**

ABOVE **Architects such as Frank Lloyd Wright made the hearth the nucleus of the home. If there is a comparable sacred spot in a Neutra house, it is the terrace—preferably with radiant heating.**
TOP LEFT **Original Neutra details that have been preserved include the taut piano wires used to form the balustrade around the deck.**
ABOVE LEFT **The transition from deck to living room is marked by a change of texture in the floor covering.**

ABOVE AND ABOVE RIGHT
Furnishings and details are very much in the spirit of Neutra's elegant functionalism, and complement the spare, simple interior.
OPPOSITE **Sliding glass doors extend the living space onto the deck, allowing owners and guests to make the most of California's equable climate.**

In a Neutra house, the relationship between indoors and out is charged with ambiguity.

Neutra was a visionary architect. He saw huge opportunities to adapt techniques of standardization from industry and exploit lightweight materials such as steel and glass to create flexible spaces and structures. Over decades, he developed and refined a family of details. Some, such as metal casement windows, remained a permanent feature in his kit-of-parts and were used in both lavish and modest projects. Early in the 1950s, he began to incorporate aluminum casement windows, restricting them to the more private parts of the house, such as kitchens or bedrooms, and using large sheets of glass to enclose living areas.

The 1950s ushered in a golden era of relaxed, sophisticated houses, in which the potential of lightweight steel frames and glass walls, reflecting pools, and remarkable sites, was explored to marvelous effect. In 1959, Neutra completed a house for a Los Angeles couple on a dramatic sloping site. The two-story house, restored in the spirit of the

original architecture by Marmol Radziner, is an imaginative fusion of space on a tight, precipitous plot on the hills above West Hollywood. Cascading down the hill, the house is dug into the site and entered from the upper floor at street level. The facade is clearly assigned two roles—private and public.

Set in the center of the house between the carport and private wing, the glazed public entrance offers tantalizing views of the living area beyond. The carport's deep overhang is supported by a row of slim tubular-steel columns plated with chrome. The sleeping areas are screened by a white wall plane, and slatted redwood siding adds a rustic touch.

Enhancing the sociability and cheerfulness of the house, the carport doubles as an outdoor living area. On the backyard side, a long balcony and deck are accessible from the living space and master bedroom via sliding glass doors. From this magnificently

elevated vantage point, Los Angeles unfolds languidly below. The overhanging roof offers additional shade and shelter. Innovative details include taut piano wires used to separate the living room from the open stairwell, a detail echoed in the rear balcony balustrades. The strong verticality of this detail is emphasized in the rhythm of the redwood siding.

Neutra's views on nature had important consequences for his dwellings. To Frank Lloyd Wright, the nucleus of the home was the hearth. To Neutra, it was the terrace—with the result that the relationship between indoors and outdoors in a Neutra house becomes charged with ambiguity. The boundary between indoors and out is marked only by a thin sheet of glass, so that nothing can interfere with the potent and primal relationship between people and nature, whether it is the benign setting of suburbia or the awesome grandeur of the California

ABOVE **The hilly topography of the site means that houses could be designed to be tucked into the slope, providing the occupants with both privacy and good views. The Neutra house opens up to the rear, overlooking a garden and the wider city beyond. The architect's interiors reveal his skill in delicately layering spatial transitions. In this case, the entire city becomes a backdrop for the daily dramas of domestic life.**

desert. Many of Neutra's houses present a similarly hermetic face to the street, providing only high strips of windows at the front, while opening out to gardens at the rear. Often the hilly topography of the site provides privacy, so houses can be tucked into slopes, which also serves to maximize views. Neutra's interiors reveal his skill in delicately layering spatial transitions. Just as he layered space, he also layered functions. As he once said, more hopefully than realistically: "In our house, rooms have no names such as living room, dining room, bedroom. Rooms are portions of a great organic living space and pragmatically elastic."

This notion of a great living space evokes the Japanese concept of the *zashiki* or principal flexible room used for living, sleeping, and entertaining. In Neutra's hands, this lyrically reinterpreted for the hedonistic lifestyles of southern California.

ABOVE RIGHT **The West Hollywood Hills offer some of the best views in the city, and breathtaking cityscapes are mirrored in the glass walls, generating a magical interplay of reflections. Richard Neutra's predilection for architecture that exploited industrial methods of mass production meant that his houses could be built quickly and economically. Standard kits-of-parts were used, leaving him free to devote more time to clients. His houses proved extremely popular and have come to epitomize a period of languid, hedonistic California Modernism.**
RIGHT **A cool cat surveys the panorama of Los Angeles.**

Interiors have a spare yet elegant quality, and simple furnishings and textures have been carefully chosen to enhance Neutra's wonderfully realized interaction of fluid space and reflected light.

THIS PICTURE **Long bands of glazing illuminate the master bedroom on the lower floor that overlooks the backyard, giving rise to sleek, simple elevations. The style of furniture adds to the sense of modern elegance.**
RIGHT, TOP TO BOTTOM
The staircase that links the two levels of the house was designed in response to the sloping site. Neutra placed the living space on the upper level, with the bedroom below. Despite this reversal of the conventional arrangement, the plan is lucid and logical, with free-flowing spaces.

Transparent townhouse

ARCHITECTS: **OGAWA & DEPARDON**

The townhouse is one of the basic building blocks of the city. Set on a narrow front-to-back plan defined by two parallel party walls and vertically oriented circulation, it is usually three to five storys high, representing the maximum comfortable climb by a fit person. It is thus intimately related to human scale, yet also part of the larger urban fabric. It is a distinct entity and at the same time a modular, replicable unit that can be combined and extended to create a variety of urban configurations. The townhouse embodies many important issues that concern architects today, such as the nature of the dialogue between individual buildings and the city as a whole, the tension between public face and private interior, and the relationship between city and suburbia—all acted out within the formal typology of the prismatic box.

The form and organization of the contemporary townhouse can be traced to a multitude of sources: the dwellings of ancient Rome, traditional London and Paris houses, the Italian palazzi, and their progeny in the work of modern masters such as Le Corbusier and Chareau. By definition, townhouses tend to be tightly enclosed and located on sites that are scarcely adequate for their programs. Adjoining buildings crowd out light as well as space. The small footprint usually dictates somewhat awkward interior arrangements, with rooms often piled up vertically. There is rarely more than one facade to design and even that, given the zoning restrictions that apply in many urban areas, cannot be conceived with total lack of inhibition. But, despite the constraints—or perhaps because of them—the townhouse has become the vehicle for a remarkable amount of innovative architecture.

For all the historical evidence that it reached its height in Georgian London and 19th-century New York, the townhouse is also very much a building of the 20th and 21st centuries, and it is undergoing a quiet yet significant revival. The lack of critical attention focused on this revival is perhaps understandable. In an age that prizes flamboyant

LEFT **The ground-floor dining area opens onto a secluded walled courtyard—a rare example of a private backyard in New York City. Limestone paving extends indoors and throughout the house.**
LEFT, INSET **Earlier apartment buildings are reflected in the sheer glass membrane enclosing the rear extension.**
ABOVE AND LEFT **Uninhibited by the zoning constraints that applied to the street frontage, the architects adopted a more expressive contemporary language in the steel-and-glass extension at the rear, which opens up the building to light and views. The taut geometry of clear glass and structural steel provides a crisply modern counterpoint to the surrounding opaque mass of the brick apartment houses.**

A series of fluid airy spaces, saturated with natural light, have been imaginatively inserted within the inflexible confines of the existing long, narrow plan.

architectural expression, it is hardly surprising that freestanding houses in the countryside attract more public interest than the townhouse, typically cramped and confined in an urban street.

Although the townhouse puts some constraints on architectural freedom, it also offers great creative potential. Indeed, some of the best houses of the last three centuries were townhouses. These include the great English architect John Soane's own labyrinthine London residence, built in the early 19th century, and the iconic Maison de Verre by Pierre Chareau, completed in 1931, which ingeniously exploited a small Parisian courtyard and was also notable for its pioneering use of glass blocks to create a gauzily translucent facade that admitted light but also maintained a degree of seclusion (see pages 12–13).

Ogawa & Depardon's remodeling of a New York townhouse represents the triumphant transformation of a gloomy old building into a chalice of light. The project involved the total gutting and reconstruction of a 19th-century Upper East Side building for clients relocating to the city from out of state.

The clients sought to recreate in the city the same kind of large, airy, light-filled living space that they were leaving behind in the suburbs. Moving to a traditional townhouse with windows only on the narrow northern and southern facades was a big change from their previous residence. They wanted an open-plan, purpose-designed house with copious natural light. Drastic modifications to the street

frontage were prohibited by the New York City Landmarks Commission, so the simple geometry of rectangular windows set in a limestone wall make the house an unassuming neighbor. But beyond this modest public face is an expansive, lofty interior, saturated with natural light. Spatial organization follows the standard townhouse arrangement in which the ground floor is given over to the kitchen, with dining and living rooms on the floor above, and bedrooms located on the two upper levels. A generously proportioned master bathroom takes up the entire width of the top floor on the street side.

Although the spatial arrangement is traditional, the manipulation of natural light has been conceived from a thoroughly modern standpoint. A sky-lit atrium containing a staircase is positioned at the heart of the long thin plan, far away from any existing source of natural light. Enclosed by large sheets of

transparent and translucent glass, the atrium is flooded with daylight, which infuses the spaces with a soft radiance. The character and intensity of the light changes with the type of glass used. Mechanical shafts, dumb waiters, closets, and other storage areas are all pulled to the building's western party wall and stacked vertically, maximizing the openness and fluidity of the plan.

Natural light also enters from the rear extension, where a new full-height volume of steel and glass connects with a secluded walled garden, landscaped in an austerely minimalist style. The protruding side walls of the two upper floors are also partially inset with glass blocks, enhancing light penetration to the bedrooms, while preserving privacy. At night, the soaring glass wall glows softly with light, a luminous and dramatic urban beacon.

The existing street frontage was stripped of its extraneous ornament to maintain continuity between the new interior and the extension. The base of the facade was covered in French limestone, a material also used in the rear yard and as flooring throughout the house. A skylight at the uppermost level of the stairwell also functions as the glass floor of an external courtyard that leads to a roof garden. This courtyard connects the master bedroom with the bathroom on the top floor.

With its crisply detailed steel-and-glass extension, the rear of the house is distinctly different from the surrounding buildings. In this more private realm, which is not at the mercy of zoning laws, the extreme contrast between the brick facades of neighboring apartment buildings and the taut grid of clear glass and dark-gray steel makes for urban drama of the highest order. Such contrasts fuel the architectural vigor of the building: openness versus enclosure, the radiance of light from the

Despite the constraints imposed by its form and location—or perhaps because of them—the townhouse has become the vehicle for a remarkable amount of innovative architecture.

OPPOSITE **Within the rigid confines of the plan form, the architects have created a series of fluid, luminous open spaces.**
LEFT AND ABOVE **The stairwell is drenched in natural light flooding in from the skylight directly above it.**
TOP **Enclosed by clear-glass panels, the stairwell can be glimpsed from different spaces within the house.**

The master bedroom occupies the top floor of the new steel-and-glass extension to the rear. Spatial organization follows the traditional arrangement of the New York townhouse, with kitchen at ground level, living spaces on the next floor, and two floors of bedrooms above. Although the plan form is conventional, the handling of space and light is imbued with a strong contemporary sensibility. In the bedroom, glass is used to diffuse light and provide privacy. Panels of clear and translucent glass form an alternating transparent and pellucid skin across one end of the room. Glass blocks are also used to open up the side walls and admit light, while preserving privacy in the cramped and overlooked urban setting.

glass against the opaque mass of the nearby masonry, and the heaviness of the brick-bearing walls counterpoised with the slender steel structure. A reciprocal dynamic is achieved between the bold new elements themselves, strengthened by their juxtaposition with the historic fabric and the existing elements. Through the harmonious and skillful conjunction of these disparate elements, Ogawa & Depardon have achieved an outstanding architectural and urban unity.

Drawing its vigor from the juxtaposition of new and existing elements, the house is a striking synthesis of space and light.

ABOVE AND OPPOSITE
The generously proportioned master bathroom on the street side of the top floor is directly connected to the master bedroom at the rear of the house.
RIGHT **Translucent glass windows are patterned with clear-glass circles to give views out and preserve a sense of seclusion. Materials and furnishings throughout the house have been carefully chosen to complement the inventive architecture, and contribute to the creation of an elegant whole.**

Parisian atelier

ARCHITECT: **DAMIEN ROLAND**

Paris is, historically, a city of apartment dwellers. The most common form of housing is the traditional walk-up apartment arranged around a central courtyard, which has come to dictate the scale and grain of the city. Individual houses are relative rarities, but occasionally the opportunity arises to create a different sort of dwelling, either by designing a completely new building or, more likely, by adapting or converting an existing structure. Damien Roland's remodeling of an unused 19th-century storeroom into a stunning space for living and working shows how a neglected building can be revived with the use of imagination and flair.

The site of Roland's conversion lies right in the heart of Paris. Surrounded by an apartment building, the storeroom sits in a cobbled courtyard filled with trees. The site has an intriguing history; the apartment was built in the late 19th century using stone from the Bastille prison, torn down by the populace during the French Revolution. Simple and functional, the storeroom was originally a single-story structure with a pitched roof. When the entire block was sold by its owner, Damien Roland saw the potential for remodeling and seized his chance.

Through inventive reconfiguration of the original compact plan, Roland has transformed the building into a three-storey house combined with a studio. Glass plays an important part in the design strategy, opening up the building in order to introduce light to the various rooms. The main problem with the

An unassuming building in the heart of Paris is transformed into a luminous living and work space through the inventive use of glass.

original area was its lack of space. Unable to extend the building upward because of zoning restrictions, Roland was obliged to work within the confines of the shell. Yet he has managed to create more space by extending the building downward, adding a subterranean basement level. Within the volume of the original shell, he has also added a mezzanine floor, so the single-story building now consists of three floors, linked by a spiral staircase which slots neatly into the tight plan without taking up a great deal of space.

When Roland first embarked on the project, he thought he might acquire the converted building for his own use, so the reorganization of the space reflects the needs of an architect living and working under one roof. The basement was designated as

OPPOSITE **The remodeled house was originally a 19th-century store and its architect makes inventive use of a compact plan. New openings are punched into the walls and roof in order to bring light into the interior. The house sits in a tree-planted courtyard, so despite its urban setting there is some contact with nature.**
RIGHT AND ABOVE RIGHT **The view down from the mezzanine level shows details of the glass floor in the living space.**
ABOVE **A chair made from clear plastic forms part of an idiosyncratic array of furniture and objects.**

a work studio, the ground floor as living quarters, with sleeping spaces above in the mezzanine. In the end, the building has been occupied by a fashion designer, but the space works just as well. The basement is now a workshop where samples are made up, the ground floor is a living and studio space, with sleeping quarters above.

To bring light into what was originally a blind box, Roland has made extensive use of glass. New glazed openings have been punched into the walls and roof, so that light floods down into the double-height living area. A new circular window is positioned over the wood-and-glass sliding doors of the entrance.

at times disarming, but the practical benefits of bringing natural light into what would have been a dingy space outweigh the momentary discomfiture.

The notion of incorporating glass into floors might appear slightly incongruous, as the material's fragility and texture would seem to make it inherently unsuitable for such an application. Yet glass floors allow the transmission of light into windowless or underground spaces. Originally conceived as a means of admitting light to staff quarters and storage areas, pavement lights made of glass blocks are a common sight in most cities. Advances in glazing technology have given rise to laminated glass,

The original volume has been remodelled to provide three floors. Visual and spatial connections between the various levels are enhanced by the use of glass.

The window can be opened in order to bring larger pieces of furniture into the house. A small sliding gantry runs along the underside of the roof to assist in this process. Roland had envisaged that the building might be used by an artist or sculptor, who might need a means of access for large-scale artworks.

The walls of the upper mezzanine level are also made of glass, giving views out over the living space and enhancing the transmission of light. But perhaps the project's most striking use of the material is in the floor of the living space. A large section of the floor is infilled with glass, so the basement workshop can obtain some natural light. The central portion of the floor is made from panels of clear glass, surrounded by a grid of translucent glass blocks, which admit light but maintain a degree of privacy. The effect is

which has great strength derived from fusing individual layers together so that it can be employed in staircases and floors.

Despite its confined urban setting, the remodeled building manages to achieve some connection with nature. The cobbled courtyard is full of trees, which form a delicate green canopy around the house. This is supplemented by a newly planted grove of bamboo that screens a large window on the ground floor overlooking the courtyard. At night the house is transformed into a glowing lantern that illuminates the entire courtyard with a soft radiance. Combining an imaginative approach to the use of space with an assured handling of materials, especially glass, Roland's inventive remodeling reinvigorates a secret urban courtyard.

A grove of bamboo frames a window in the living quarters, which are also used as studio space. The thin, leafy shoots cast rippling shadows on the surrounding walls, which are predominantly white, enhancing a sense of lightness. The house's compact plan and clean, minimal aesthetic evoke the elemental simplicity of traditional Japanese dwellings. Concealed in an urban courtyard, it waits to reveal its delights.

Light and space in suburbia

ARCHITECTS: **MACK SCOGIN MERRILL ELAM**

Tucked between downtown Atlanta and the affluent Buckhead district are the leafy streets of Brookwood Hills, a planned residential community dating from the 1920s. While Brookwood's community swimming pool draws its fair share of attention during the summer months, it is the structure across the street, the house of architects Mack Scogin and Merrill Elam, that is the focus of envious attention all year round. On the second floor, wrapped in screens of milky glass, is a narrow lap pool. Passersby can hear the splashing when the pool is in use, but cannot see the bathers— and, unlike the public pool, no swimsuit is required.

Scogin and Elam have lived in the neighborhood since 1976, when they bought a steep-roofed bungalow, not for its architectural merits, but for its modest price and desirable location midway between Atlanta's inner city and suburbs. Merrill Elam hated the original house—so much so that, on moving in, she took a sledgehammer to the walls between the tiny rooms. If the desire for a new architectural order was apparent from the moment the architects moved in, it took time, an accumulation of resources, and some surprising twists of fate to make their imagined changes real. For nearly 20 years, Scogin and Elam lived in their bungalow, making only modest renovations—a streamlined interior plan and the addition of two small guest pavilions in the backyard.

In 1995, nature intervened, when a tree blown down in a hurricane crashed through the roof of the house, landing in the couple's bed. Fortunately, they were both in their apartment in Cambridge, Massachusetts, where Scogin was teaching at Harvard's Graduate School of Design. Twice before, trees had fallen on the house, but this was the first time that one had actually fallen into it. The house was completely destroyed; the tree had split the walls and cracked the ridge beam of the roof. (It took 15 men two days just to remove it.) At first, the architects camped out in the remnants of their home, planning to rebuild it largely as it had been. Then Merrill Elam had an epiphany and decided that she wanted a lap pool. It became the couple's grand obsession and dictated the course of plans for the new house.

From the street, the house is decidedly enigmatic, a curious presence among the more conventional bungalows and split-levels. The facade's geometric composition is dominated by the strong horizontal planes of the lap pool on the second floor.

The living space is located on the south-facing street side of the house, to take advantage of light and views. Taut planes of frameless clear glass resembling a store window are set against the heaviness and solidity of concrete. A staircase with open risers leads to the bedroom and pool on the second floor.

THIS PICTURE **Defined by white wall planes, the living area is a series of fluid, open-plan spaces. The overlapping areas are not conceived as a series of planned rooms, but rather as a choreography of movement. The exposed steel beams are a visual joke—they have no structural function.**

A spirit of ambiguity constantly plays against expectations,
finding coherence in the seemingly absurd collage of spaces.

The site faces south across the street, with views towards the neighborhood park and tennis courts, with hills beyond. Fueled by dreams of exercise and relaxation, the idea of the lap pool provided the impetus for the design. Finding a place to put it was not easy, however. The backyard was occupied by two guest pavilions, leaving no room to maneuver, and local zoning laws prohibited siting a pool in the front yard. Eventually the architects decided to put it on the upper story of the new house. The only way the site could accommodate the 50ft- (15m-) long pool was across its width, so it was dramatically elevated to the second floor, spanning the spaces of the floor below and orientated to the south for the light. Extremely heavy and massive, the pool shell is made of on-site concrete. This varies in thickness between 1 and 2ft (25 and 50cm) around its four sides and is 1ft (25cm) deep. The shell has a deliberately rough concrete finish so its presence is expressed throughout the house. It is supported by 12ft- (3m-) deep foundations underneath the load-bearing walls.

Shielded from the street by a translucent glass wall, yet open to the sky and air, the pool challenges the notions of public and private space. Surrounded by a wooden deck, it crowns the two-floor master-bedroom, with dressing rooms and closets downstairs, and a sleeping area and bathroom above. Once the pool was designed, other living spaces were arranged around it. The laminated glass provides a gauzily translucent screen around the pool, which is animated at night by wavy patterns and mysterious reflections as the glass glows with light.

The architects regularly discussed design details with the contractors, working in an casual, "design-as-you-go" way that they relished, but would not use in formal commissions. In fact, during the house's construction, Scogin and Elam were also working on four other houses concurrently with their practice.

ABOVE **The staircase cascades down through space. Clear glass crisply frames the balustrade.**
BELOW **Books are arranged informally along a wall.**
BELOW, INSETS **Items from Scogin and Elam's collection of architect-designed chairs are displayed at various points throughout the interior.**

The firm's houses are as different as their clients, locations, uses, and budgets, but all are connected by a distinctive, expressionistic form-making, which is as much about aesthetic appeal as about constantly playing against expectations, finding coherence in the seemingly absurd collage of spaces and richness in the plainest of materials. "The house is the great experiment in American architecture," says Scogin. But in their own house, the architects went further, melding horizontal and vertical spaces into a three-dimensional pinwheel.

The deliberate ambiguity and open-endedness of rooms are increased by the reflections of the open-air pool against its shimmering glass walls. At night, the windswept pool water casts shadows on the translucent facade, animating the surface with ripples. During the day, images of trees are projected onto the concrete walls around the pool, making the structure itself appear transparent. "I wake up every morning seeing through concrete," marvels Scogin, describing the panorama of trees both real and reflected that is visible from his bed.

Some of Scogin and Elam's most memorable houses have been for dramatic rural sites, locations that have given them the freedom to experiment. By contrast, the Atlanta house had to conform to an urban context and an extremely tight site. The pool's presence and structure is clearly expressed as a broad band of rough concrete running along the facade. The massiveness of the concrete is tempered by the delicacy of the translucent glass wall above that screens the pool from public view. Putting the pool in such a conspicuous position is a highly unconventional move that flies in the face of the American suburban norm of the pool discreetly tucked into a backyard corner. In this case the pool addresses the public realm, but is still a private space. The only tantalizing clues to its presence are the sounds of splashing and ripples of light reflected off the water onto the translucent glass screen. At some stage, Elam hopes to plant a bamboo grove in the front yard to shield the house from the street.

Inside, the pool structure forms the ceiling to the living quarters below, but despite its physical massiveness, it does not feel heavy. Guests sit in the living room underneath the pool tank without

FAR LEFT AND THIS PICTURE
The open risers allow views through the staircase as it darts between floors.
FAR LEFT, INSET **Leather club chairs, originally designed by Le Corbusier, frame a doorway.**
ABOVE LEFT **The heavy-duty kitchen sink is suspended from the ceiling by a series of thin rods. The kitchen is placed at the rear of the house, overlooking the guest pavilions.**
BELOW LEFT **Wall planes dissolve spaces. Walls are predominantly white, with wood-fibrous cement flooring panels laid on top of the concrete floor structure.**

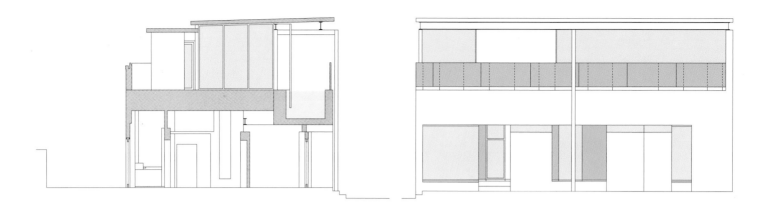

flinching. Scogin and Elam relish this paradox between lightness and heaviness, which is a consistent theme of their architecture. They allude to the great domes of European classical architecture, such as the Pantheon in Rome, which although physically heavy, achieve a certain lightness of experience. Likewise, the pool's great mass seems to float through the space of the house.

On the second floor, the glazed pavilion of the bedroom directly overlooks the narrow strip of seductively blue water, separated from it by an insubstantial membrane of clear glass. Throughout the house, glass is set against more massive elements, creating surprising juxtapositions, revealing views and bringing light to the interior. Sheer planes of clear, frameless glass are also used to form balustrades around the stairs and landings. The glass is detailed with a great precision, so that it appears seamless and floating, enhancing a sense of lightness and dematerialization. Walls are predominantly white, with wood-fibrous cement flooring panels laid on top of the concrete floor structure. The smooth texture of the floors and walls forms a resonant contrast with the rough concrete of the pool. Exposed steel beams appear intermittently throughout the interior, ostensibly as a dramatic expression of structure, but in fact as mere

ABOVE LEFT **A cross section shows how the pool is supported at first-floor level. Elevating the pool was an unorthodox solution, but lack of space gave the architects no alternative. The pool shell is made of concrete, which varies in thickness around its four sides. It is supported by deep foundations underneath the load-bearing walls. The underside of the pool forms the ceiling of the living area, but despite its heavy physical presence, it achieves a certain lightness of experience.**
ABOVE RIGHT **The strong horizontal planes of the lap pool dominate the geometric composition of the facade.**

connects the main house with the guest pavilions. The second floor is entirely devoted to the bedroom, the pool, and its deck, a sybaritic den of luxury. But both Scogin and Elam are by nature workaholics. "They do architecture all day," according to their partner Lloyd Bray. Does this make them immune to the distracting pleasures of the house? "Well maybe they wake up in the morning and take a quick swim. And then they do architecture all day."

Being based in Atlanta has given Scogin and Elam's practice a certain freshness and originality of vision. The quintessential American suburban city spreading out in tree-lined streets, Atlanta is still evolving and still, in many ways, searching for some kind of identity. This quality of undefinability underscores the work of the practice. Free from the encumbrances of history, context, and the architectural politics of the East and West Coasts, they have been able to develop their own vision and approach. Atlanta's relative youth colors the city's perception of architecture as evolving and experimental, rather than a precious and untouchable historical commodity.

Mack Scogin Merrill Elam Architects cultivate their sensibilities to the point where they can do with architecture what is usually thought of as beyond the realms of architecture: capturing and exploring different possibilties. One critic has described it as "a

Throughout the house, clear and translucent glass is set against more massive elements, creating surprising juxtapositions.

decoration, an example of architectural playfulness. Furnishings consist mainly of Scogin and Elam's collection of architect-designed chairs that are arranged like sculptures around the house.

The plan is a fluid series of spaces contained and locked together within the rectangular footprint of the site. The living space is placed on the south-facing street side, to take advantage of the sun. Kitchen and laundry rooms are located at the rear, overlooking the two self-contained guest pavilions that occupy the garden. A bridgelike library at second-floor level

sort of embraced madness." They do not necessarily begin with the proper and the inevitable. Their outlook is sometimes more challenging and less manageable. But neither do they set out to change the conventions of architecture, to ignore the fact that architects must create buildings with use and meaning. Instead, they augment architecture with the enduring lessons of the irregular. Projects such as their own extraordinary house are the outcome of mixing together what they know architecture can do and what, in their wildest speculations, they think may be possible.

THIS PICTURE **A piece of wood forms an impromptu shelf, suspended between the pool enclosure and the bedroom's built-in television cabinet.**

TOP RIGHT **Junctions between glass panels are detailed with seamless precision.**

CENTER RIGHT **Seen from below, the wooden shelf seems to hover in space.**

BOTTOM RIGHT **The interior geometry of solid and void is one of the most distinctive features of the house.**

THIS PICTURE AND TOP LEFT
The bedroom is a glazed pavilion overlooking the enticing strip of water. The pool addresses the public realm, but is still a private space, enclosed by a screen of translucent glass. Water casts rippling reflections on the underside of the cantilevered roof, which protects and shades the pool.
CENTER LEFT **Bedroom and pool merge into one fluid volume.**
BOTTOM LEFT **There is no visual clue to the pool's presence from the street.**

The idea of glass as a beautiful material in its own right finds expression in the work of many contemporary architects and designers. Glass and glazing technology has become increasingly sophisticated, with the potential to create an amazing range of interior effects. Dramatic or subtle contrasts between light and shadow, opacity and transparency, can be realized through the imaginative use of different sorts of glass. Glass can be used in floors, walls, roofs, for internal screens, even in staircases, creating scintillating cascades of light and dematerializing solid volumes. Glass in floors has evolved from robust pavement lights to discreet panels that bring light through to lower levels, opening up both new and existing dwellings in different ways. Glass screens can be used to enclose and define space, creating privacy when required. This concluding chapter is a celebration of glass's enormous diversity, focusing on how even the most modest glass features and elements can bring an interior to life. From Simon Conder's daring translucent bathroom pods to Rick Mather's weightless, transparent staircase, the visual appeal and sensual allure of this most versatile of materials can be enjoyed in a multitude of forms.

Glass endows functional domestic spaces with a sculptural quality, introducing a sense of grace and lightness to rooms. In this compact bathroom, the washbasin takes the form of a glass bowl sunk into a glazed unit, and the bathtub is a simple rectangular box that barely seems to be there.

LEFT **A glazed rear extension has opened up this Georgian house in London, remodeled by Azman Owens. Mild steel grilles, resembling a modern version of traditional Turkish screens, provide privacy.**
THIS PAGE **Full-height clear-glass walls enclose the kitchen. Units are set in a freestanding frame, so as not to obstruct the light that comes through the walls and illumines the many pieces of contemporary art in the house.**

Walls and floors

The notion of glass as a beautiful material in its own right was a tenet of early 20th-century Modernism and finds continued expression today in the work of many contemporary architects and designers. The increasing sophistication of glass and glazing technology has made possible an amazing range of effects. Powerful contrasts between light and shadow, and between transparency and opacity, can be realized through the skillful and imaginative use of glass in walls, internal screens, and even floors. Modernism is most commonly associated with the use of clear glass, but many architects are now using translucent glass in a reinterpretation of the Japanese tradition of filtering light through rice-paper screens known as *shoji*.

Azman Owens' remodeling of a traditional row house in south London is a subtle and inventive exploitation of the different properties of glass. With its dollhouse proportions and modest exterior, this Georgian dwelling is part of a row built as workers' cottages in 1826. When the house was acquired by its current owners it was completely unmodernized, with small, dark rooms; there was no kitchen and, apart from an outside toilet, no bathroom.

Azman Owens proposed a two-story glass extension that stacks the bathroom over the kitchen while encouraging daylight to penetrate the interior. The lightweight steel-and-glass addition replaces a single-story lean-to shed tacked onto the rear elevation. A spirit of simplicity and economy prevails. Inventive use of materials and a sensitive response to scale has resulted in an extension that sits comfortably with the original building.

To flood the house with light, Azman Owens inserted glazed slots and opened up the interior to create framed views through rooms and out into the garden. For privacy without the loss of daylight, the bathroom—on the upper floor of the extension—is partially screened by an external steel grid. For architect Ferhan Azman the device recalls traditional Turkish hinged shutters in her native Istanbul, where streets are so narrow that houses are cantilevered to increase light penetration; for privacy, wooden grilles

ABOVE **This new conservatory for a London house is a minimal composition of glass and white wall planes.**
OPPOSITE **The double-height volume, flooded with daylight, mediates between the interior and exterior of the house. Enhancing the sense of lightness and ethereality, the clear-glass roof is supported by laminated glass beams. Tall glass walls are detailed with a seamless precision.**

resembling ladders are added to the exterior. In this case, the metal grilles act like a stylish modern equivalent of sheer curtains.

Made from prerusted steel applied with a clear polyester coating, the grilles add texture to the house and blend with the existing brickwork. A limited palette of materials helps to unify the interior and exterior. The mild steel of the grilles is also employed on surfaces inside the house, its gently tarnished finish providing a more sensual alternative to stainless steel. Kitchen cabinets have been wrapped in mild steel and sealed with a clear varnish.

At one point, the boundary between art and architecture is seductively blurred: floorboards are replaced with glazed strips to encourage the transmission of light into the basement. Directly below the glass slots is an installation by fine-art graduate Ben Currow consisting of a sealed tank filled with water that subtly vibrates to cast shimmering shadows on the walls.

One obvious way to introduce light into the compact, cellular plans of older urban houses is to add some kind of glass conservatory or winter garden. Mark Guard's refurbishment of a Victorian house in western

The increasing sophistication of glass and glazing technology has given rise to an astonishingly diverse range of effects.

The house contains numerous clues to its owners' flamboyant natures and their love of contemporary art. Next to the bathroom, with its delicate glass washbasin and glass bathtub, is a dressing room containing an extraordinary collection of hats and shoes. These sculptural creations are displayed in exquisitely designed glass cases, transforming the room into an idiosyncratic gallery. An open glazed slit incised into the bedroom wall permits glimpses of the garden beyond. Objects from the couple's collection of contemporary art are placed around the house, giving rise to moments of surprise and delight.

London is a highly sophisticated example of this familiar practice. Through a series of resourceful domestic conversions, mainly in London, Guard has acquired a reputation for buildings that combine calm, neutral spaces with a finely honed material sense. In this house, the rear wall has been opened up through a tall conservatory, replacing a former utility room. The new extension adopts the traditional "lean-to" form, but its clear-glass walls are distinguished by their seamlessness and precision. More remarkably, the glass roof is supported by beams made of laminated glass, continuing Guard's

THIS PICTURE A translucent glass wall in the Harry House, designed by William Heffner, recalls a Japanese rice-paper screen, a device whose effect combines an exquisite quality of light with privacy. Light is diffused through sandblasted glass panels to fill the room with a gentle radiance.
INSET A bar in the Harry House combines mirrors with translucent glass lit from behind to animate the surface, thereby creating a scintillating play of light.

ABOVE AND RIGHT **Sheer clear-glass walls enclose the living room of the Harry House, dissolving the boundaries between inside and out. An external terrace can be used to extend the living space in warm weather. Over the past 20 years, the art and science of transparency has been pushed to new boundaries by architects eager to exploit new siding materials and anchoring technologies with the same pioneering zeal as their predecessors did in the 1920s and 1930s. Domestic architecture forms an ideal testbed for experiments.**

Forming a diaphanous membrane between inside and out, clear-glass walls open up interior spaces.

theme of achieving architectural refinement by exploiting the latest advances in glass technology.

As architects and designers discovered long ago, the use of glazed walls and screens can elegantly reconcile the visual and the functional requirements of interior spaces. William Heffner's Harry House in West Hollywood is infused with a calm, elemental radiance gently diffused through translucent glass walls. His poetic handling of light is emphasized by his sensuous treatment of the interior, in which reflective surfaces of luxurious materials enhance the play of light.

By contrast, Simon Conder's conversion of a 19th-century warehouse in London's East End into a loft apartment responds to the stark quality of an existing industrial building by stripping the interior down to its barest essentials. Conder's austere

ABOVE AND RIGHT **Glass has been used in many delightful ways in Simon Conder's conversion in London's East End, of a 19th-century warehouse into a spacious loft apartment. Where the original building shell was double height, a sleeping gallery has been inserted at upper level, in the form of a glass box surrounded by a roof terrace. A staircase links the sleeping gallery with a living room.**
TOP **The living room shows how Conder's architectural style responds to the stark quality of an existing building by stripping down the interior to its bare essentials.**

sensibilities—his pleasure in clear, unobstructed space and a few carefully chosen materials—have been consistently demonstrated in a succession of recent projects. In this instance, he retains the L-shaped building shell as a single volume for living, cooking, and dining, and opens it up to the west with sliding glass doors giving onto a terrace. A sleeping gallery in the form of a glass box surrounded by a second, larger roof terrace has been installed on the upper level; it resembles a transparent eyrie floating loftily above the London skyline. A sandblasted glass and acrylic bridge connects the gallery with a simple flight of oak stairs leading to the living space below. At night, light filters through the bridge, generating a soft, seductive glow. Bathrooms are replaced by a pair of freestanding translucent glass drums, which are another source of nighttime illumination.

The notion of incorporating glass into floors might seem, slightly incongruous. Yet it makes possible the transmission of light into windowless or underground spaces. Originally conceived as a means of admitting light to staff quarters and storage areas, pavement lights made of glass blocks remain a common sight in most cities. In Azman Owens' house conversion, strips of clear glass were inserted into the wood floor

Glass floors allow light to pass vertically through interiors, and give surprising and disarming glimpses of lower levels.

so light could penetrate through the compact plan. In the house designed by Rick Mather in north London, the transmission of light is enhanced not only by large areas of glass in the walls and roof, but also by toughened panels set in the floor.

Mather's work is characterized by fluidly interpenetrating spaces, animated and energized by the presence of light. In this case, light floods down through a huge glass roof, bathing the living area in a brilliant radiance. Glass heightens the connection with the outside, and occupants are aware of every nuance of the changing weather and light. The glazed floor sections trap and filter light down to a pool in the basement, giving glimpses of the mysterious water-filled cavern below. At times, the effect is slightly disarming, as the floor seems to disappear under your feet, creating the illusion that you are walking on air. Light shimmers and scintillates in the pool, casting dappled reflections around the subterranean space.

Without glass to open up space and transmit light, none of these effects would have been possible. In the hands of accomplished designers, glass in its many forms brings the spatial drama of architecture vividly to life.

LEFT **Rick Mather's use of glass in this London house creates a disarming transparency. Glazed floor panels give views down to the swimming pool on the lowest level. Light shimmers off the water and glass to create a gauzy play of reflections.** ABOVE, FAR LEFT **Glazed slits in the floorboards of the house bring light down through the various levels and allow glimpses of the floors below.** BELOW, FAR LEFT AND CENTER **Glass was also used in Azman Owens' conversion of a Georgian house in London. Toughened-glass panels set in the wood floor transmit light down into the basement, while glass-covered uplighters give gentle illumination.**

Staircases

A crystalline glass staircase is the focus of a house conversion in London by architect Alan Power. The luminous slot of the stairwell is incised into the house, bringing light down into its lower levels. The house itself is reorganized to create open-plan volumes instead of a series of cellular rooms. Each glass tread has been dot-fritted to provide grip.

Throughout the history of building, stairs have played a crucial part in the creation of spatial and formal relationships, and for architects they are the supreme test of ingenuity. It might seem perverse to consider using glass in the design of a staircase. Glass is an inherently fragile and delicate material, not best suited to the rigorous structural and functional demands of such an element of the home. But technological advances, notably in the development of laminated glass, when sheets are glued or fused together to create a composite material, have endowed the material with new dimensions of strength and durability. Particularly when partnered with steel, this gives rise to often stunning flights of architectural imagination. Many architects have explored the potential of glass in staircases, attracted by its qualities of transparency and capacity to diffuse light.

The Czech-born architect and interior designer Eva Jiricna has designed over 20 staircases around the world, and her passion for certain materials, particularly metal and glass, is palpable. "Using them is like learning a language. Each time you use them again you learn a new word," she says. Her practice is well versed in the design of refined yet luxurious stores, including several for Joseph Ettedgui in London and nearly 50 for Joan & David in the U.S. One of Jiricna's earliest and most memorable commissions was for the Joseph store on Sloane Street, London. Here, a dramatic steel and glass staircase is slung between three floors, a single flight connecting each floor, replacing an existing spiral stair. In the retail spaces, glass shelves were designed to display clothes and accessories in a sparkling interior, and the staircase draws on similar themes of ephemerality and transparency.

Jiricna has also been involved in a number of house conversions. For the refurbishment of an apartment in London's Knightsbridge, as part of the scheme for unifying the space, she designed a spectacular spiral staircase that explored a similar language to that of her famous retail commissions. Consuming the minimum of space, the staircase has a transparency that allows light to filter around the house. It is beguilingly translucent and glittering, yet reassuringly solid. Spiraling up through the house, it resembles a shining steel and glass beanstalk, and its structure, like that of a plant, satisfies both functional and structural imperatives in the most economical fashion. The finely judged combination of glass treads and lacelike balustrading has a seductive, shimmering intensity.

Jiricna's staircases are small yet complex masterpieces of engineering, and she collaborates closely with structural engineers to achieve the impossibly transparent, disembodied effect she seeks. "For me a staircase is an opportunity for invention and escapism," she says. It is also proof that modern design methods can compete with the craftsmanship of the 19th century.

Other contemporary architects strive to achieve a less consciously engineered aesthetic, preferring instead to emphasize the purity and refinement of glass. An extraordinary staircase designed by Alan

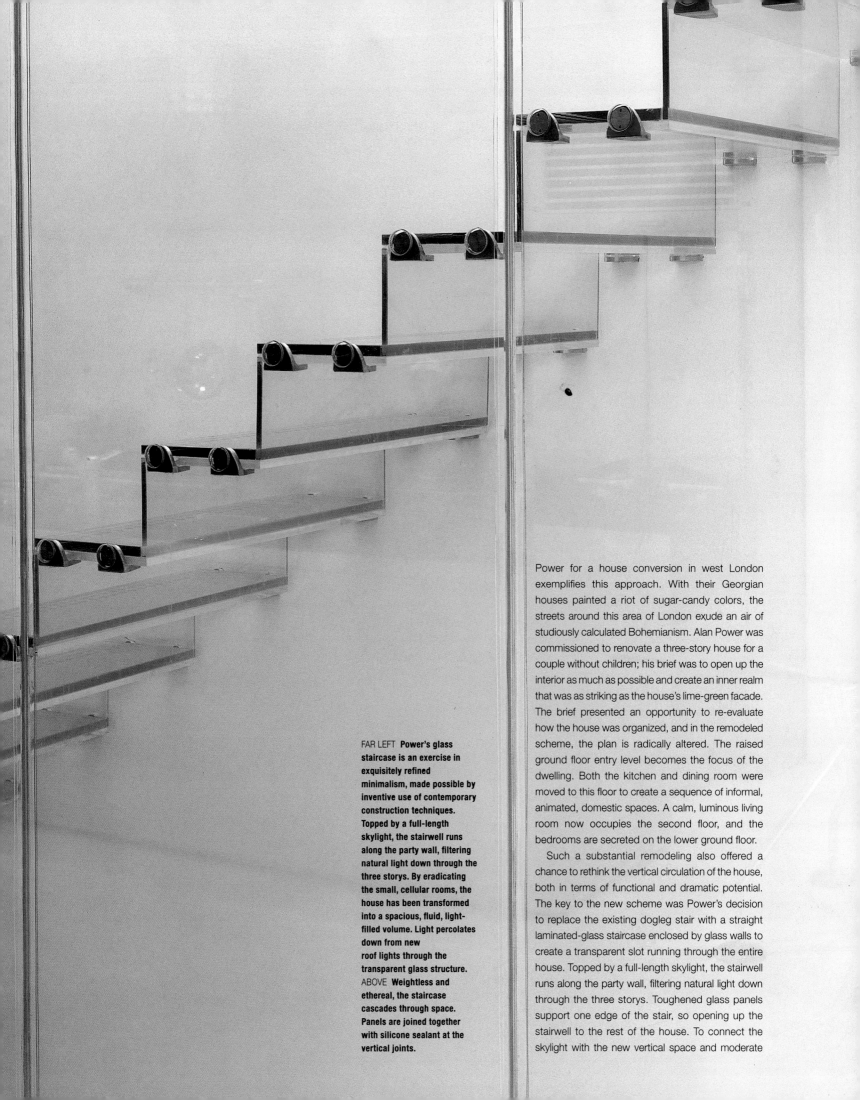

FAR LEFT **Power's glass staircase is an exercise in exquisitely refined minimalism, made possible by inventive use of contemporary construction techniques. Topped by a full-length skylight, the stairwell runs along the party wall, filtering natural light down through the three storys. By eradicating the small, cellular rooms, the house has been transformed into a spacious, fluid, light-filled volume. Light percolates down from new roof lights through the transparent glass structure.** ABOVE **Weightless and ethereal, the staircase cascades through space. Panels are joined together with silicone sealant at the vertical joints.**

Power for a house conversion in west London exemplifies this approach. With their Georgian houses painted a riot of sugar-candy colors, the streets around this area of London exude an air of studiously calculated Bohemianism. Alan Power was commissioned to renovate a three-story house for a couple without children; his brief was to open up the interior as much as possible and create an inner realm that was as striking as the house's lime-green facade. The brief presented an opportunity to re-evaluate how the house was organized, and in the remodeled scheme, the plan is radically altered. The raised ground floor entry level becomes the focus of the dwelling. Both the kitchen and dining room were moved to this floor to create a sequence of informal, animated, domestic spaces. A calm, luminous living room now occupies the second floor, and the bedrooms are secreted on the lower ground floor.

Such a substantial remodeling also offered a chance to rethink the vertical circulation of the house, both in terms of functional and dramatic potential. The key to the new scheme was Power's decision to replace the existing dogleg stair with a straight laminated-glass staircase enclosed by glass walls to create a transparent slot running through the entire house. Topped by a full-length skylight, the stairwell runs along the party wall, filtering natural light down through the three storys. Toughened glass panels support one edge of the stair, so opening up the stairwell to the rest of the house. To connect the skylight with the new vertical space and moderate

ABOVE **The remodeling of this west London house presented an opportunity to re-evaluate how the house was organized. The wafer-thin glass balustrade surrounding the stairwell is detailed with meticulous precision.**
RIGHT (INSET) **Detail of blown glass lamps.**
LEFT **The glazed slot of the stairwell cuts through the house. To connect the skylight with the new vertical space and to moderate the horizontality of the original arrangement, a stair of great physical and visual lightness was required.**

the typical stacked horizontality of London row houses, a staircase of immense lightness and transparency, such as this, was required.

Linking the ground-floor dining and kitchen area with the living space at second-floor level, the new straight-flight stair is made of glass and enclosed by a glass wall. The new stair exploits the potential of laminating technology, structural silicone, and newly developed transparent structural tape.

Glass treads and risers are supported by pairs of 1⅞ x 2¾in (48 x 70mm) stainless-steel shoes, bolted at one side to a steel stringer concealed within the party wall, and on the other side to the triple-laminated clear-glass wall that encloses the stair. The wall rises up beyond the second-floor level to form a protective transparent balustrade around the

Despite their fragile properties, glass staircases have a seductive, crystalline quality and an amazing capacity to diffuse light.

stairwell. Treads are made of ¾in (19mm) clear toughened glass edge-bonded to a bottom layer of ⅝in (15mm) acrylic sheet, and the outside edge of each is dot fritted, which provides an element of visual safety as well as grip. When backlit by the low winter sun, the edges of the laminated glass glow blue-green, and the fritting casts myriad shadows on the adjacent wall. The back edge of the glass and front edge of the acrylic sheet are stopped short to provide a rebbet into which the ½in (12mm) toughened-glass

risers slot. Silicone "bubble tape" was used to bond the treads to the stainless-steel shoes.

The glass wall is a composite sandwich consisting of two sheets of ⅜in (10mm) toughened glass with a ¼in (8mm) acrylic layer bonded in between. Three 11½ft- (3.5m-) high panels are fused together with silicone sealant at the vertical joints. The wall rests on a channel set in the ground floor. At second-floor level, it is bolted to an edge beam with stainless-steel pig-nosed bolts and extends 36in (90cm) up beyond

the floor level to form a balustrade. Each glass panel in the wall was installed as a single ⅜in (10mm) glass sheet bonded to the acrylic layer, which provides reinforcement and rigidity for lateral loading. The stainless-steel shoes were bolted to the glass with stainless-steel pig-nosed bolts; larger predrilled holes in the acrylic layer allowed the bolts' heads to fit flush with it. The third layer of glass sheet was adhesive-fixed on site and the composite panels bolted to the edge beam.

The strong verticality expressed in the staircase is continued in sections of laminated glass flooring, at the head of the glass staircase at second-floor level and on the section of second floor over the front door. The staircase down to the basement is covered in limestone, with a sawtooth glass screen built into the limestone as a guard. In Georgian houses, the basements are usually dimly lit, but in this case, blue-tinged light floods down through the glass staircase from the skylight above. And, where a conventionally made staircase would have obstructed views and the flow of light, the delicate new stair induces lightness and transparency throughout the house.

Similar principles inform Rick Mather's design for a staircase in a house in north London. A core of circulation links together the house's three storys, but it also functions as a light well, bringing daylight down to the basement level, where it sparkles and refracts off a subterranean swimming pool. Light transmission is enhanced by Mather's employment of clear glass treads and risers supported by slim steel stringers. The glass dematerializes the staircase, so it seems barely there, an ethereal crystalline presence. Balustrades, both on the staircase and around the upper-level gallery, are equally minimal, consisting of thin planes of clear glass set in steel footings. This exquisite refinement of form is unencumbered by visual distractions – the top of each plane simply acts as the handrail. William Heffner also uses glass in a balustrade for a staircase for his Harry House in the Hollywood hills, but the effect is rather more ornate, recalling the designs of Frank Lloyd Wright, with sheets of translucent glass of varying sizes inserted at intervals into a steel frame. Such projects aptly demonstrate glass's remarkable versatility, and how it can play a dramatic role inside as well as out.

ABOVE AND ABOVE LEFT **The staircase of the Harry House in Hollywood, California, by William Heffner incorporates panels of translucent glass in a decorative balustrade.** OPPOSITE (MAIN PICTURE AND INSET, TOP LEFT) **In a house designed by Rick Mather in London, a beautifully detailed glass staircase links together the house's three storys. The circulation core also acts as a lightwell, introducing daylight into the basement-level swimming pool. The delicate stair reinforces the sense of lightness and dematerialization.** OPPOSITE (INSETS, BELOW) **Bladelike balustrades around the stairwell are made from thin planes of glass.**

Weaving through space, bringing light and animation, glass stairs are the ultimate combination of rigorous function and visual delight.

THIS PICTURE AND INSET
A mosaic-sided bathtub is the focus of the bathroom in William Heffner's Harry House in Hollywood. Light streams in from the translucent glass windows and is reflected through a transparent screen enclosing the tub and defining a shower area beyond. The entire space is a sumptuous conflation of light and shimmering surfaces.
OPPOSITE, BELOW **A bowllike washbasin sits elegantly poised on a bathroom cabinet in the Harry House. Mirrors capture and reflect light, animating the interior.**
OPPOSITE, ABOVE **The bathroom in Bataille & ibens' Antwerp house is an austerely functional internalized space, lined with translucent glass.**

Bathroom fixtures

Historically the most private space in a house, the bathroom has often been given scant attention in planning and design. But social and architectural attitudes change. Bathrooms are becoming sensual, light-filled havens, and architects' growing interest in these spaces reflects evolving social conventions, design trends, and environmental concerns.

In this context, the use of glass, whether in the form of screens or for fixtures, reflects both advances in glass technology and expanding horizons of the architectural imagination. The choice of glass—clear or translucent, textured or colored—can create a compelling diversity of effects, depending on the character of the space. Dramatic or subtle contrasts can be realized through combining different types of glass, some of which can be used to give a sculptural quality to items such as washbasins and bathtubs.

In William Heffner's Harry House in the Hollywood Hills, the daily ritual of bathing is celebrated in a large, luminous space animated by the shimmering and scintillating play of natural light on glass, mirrors, and mosaic tiles. Privacy and the need for light are reconciled by enclosing the bathroom in windows made of translucent glass, whose effect resembles that of Japanese rice-paper screens. The focus of the bathroom is a decadently large tub, its sides embellished with pistachio-colored mosaic tiles, which also cover some of the wall surfaces. Tall panels of delicately tinted bluish glass form a transparent screen around the tub. Light filters through the different kinds of glass and reflects off the mosaics, floor tiles, and mirrored wall surrounding the washbasin, transforming the bathroom into an oasis of tranquility devoted to sensual pleasure. Heffner's

big, luminous space contrasts with Bataille & ibens' approach to the bathroom in their house near Antwerp (see pages 30–37). Whereas Heffner takes advantage of natural light, Bataille & ibens locate the bathroom in the heart of the house, stowed away in a functional service core. The plan is meant to be highly flexible—wall partitions can be moved around to create different spatial relationships—but this internalized space is transformed by the sensitive use of glass. Walls are lined with translucent glass panels or mirrors to reflect light, so that even this confined setting has an luminous serenity.

Some architects have begun to explore the bathroom's potential as a freestanding element set in an open-plan interior. Simon Conder's remodeling of a warehouse in east London to create a loft apartment retains the shell of the building to enclose a single volume for cooking, living, and dining. Within the fluid space, a pair of translucent glass drums form a mysterious, sculptural presence. One contains a shower, the other a basin and toilet. Curved panels made of sandblasted glass slot together seamlessly. Capped by a translucent skylight set into the wooden floor of the terrace above, the drums are naturally lit during the day and a source of luminescence at night. Conder enjoys exploiting the inherent qualities of materials: the heaviness and translucence of the thickened glass, the lightness of steel, and the warmth of wood

Freestanding glass bathroom pods are now becoming the dramatic focus of many domestic interiors.

underfoot. Treating the bathroom as a freestanding pod has become something of a Conder signature. In an earlier remodeling in London's Primrose Hill, he created a stylishly minimal living space with a shower, basin, and toilet housed in a single freestanding enclosure covered with translucent glass.

Within these bathroom pods, elements such as basins and toilets are treated as intricate pieces of sculpture. With no walls to conceal services, everything is exposed and expressed, including the plumbing. In the east London loft, a frosted-glass basin seems to hover in space, reverentially served by a single faucet. Through Conder's inspired use of glass, the functional and sensual qualities of bathrooms are effortlessly reconciled.

Developments in glass technology herald even more daring erosions between public and private realms. At Bar 89 in New York, designed by Gilles Depardon of Ogawa & Depardon, toilet cubicles are disconcertingly enclosed by a transparent glass wall. When a cubicle is occupied, a closing mechanism

ABOVE AND ABOVE RIGHT
In London's East End, Simon Conder remodeled a 19th-century industrial warehouse to form a large loft apartment. The focus of the project is an open-plan living space containing a pair of bathroom pods. Circular in plan, they are enclosed by sheets of translucent glass, generating a seductive and mysterious sculptural presence. Fixtures are all exposed, and items such as shelves and towel hooks are incorporated into a single, immaculately detailed services pole.
RIGHT **Each pod is capped by a translucent roof light.**
FAR RIGHT **A glass basin appears to hover in space, and even the toilet has a polished elegance.**

THIS PICTURE **The translucent glass basin in Simon Conder's London apartment is an inventive and beautifully crafted response to function. A single faucet extending from a services pole completes the composition. The daily act of washing is celebrated and transformed into a sensuous ritual through the use of luxurious materials, the enclosure of space, and the play of light.**

Even in the most confined setting, glass in its many forms has the potential to enrich and animate space.

passes an electric current through a gel in the laminated glass and the doors become reassuringly opaque. The high cost of such devices makes them more suitable for commercial than domestic applications, but they offer a foretaste of things to come. A more conventional approach to bathroom design can be discerned in Ogawa & Depardon's New York townhouse (see pages 134–43), where the master bathroom takes up the entire width of the top floor on the street side. Translucent-glass windows are patterned with clear-glass circles to give views out and to preserve a sense of seclusion. Fixtures are beautifully detailed, reflecting the spirit of elegant austerity that pervades the entire house. Ogawa & Depardon's bathroom had the luxury of generous space; by contrast, Azman Owens' remodeling of a house in south London had to make the most effective use of a very tight plan. In this case, the bathroom is

ABOVE LEFT **Large slabs of mirror give an open feel to one corner of the master bedroom in Ogawa & Depardon's New York townhouse.**
ABOVE **In the south London house remodeled by Azman Owens, the challenge was to make the most of a small area. Transparent materials are used to filter light, and mirrors enhance the sense of space.**

set on the second floor, compactly planned to maximize the space. The washbasin is a glass bowl sunk into a glazed unit, which also acts as a partial screen between the toilet and the purpose-designed tub. The tub itself is a rectangular glass box with teak edges that can simply be lifted off when they need replacing. Mirrors are used to create a sense of space, and the limited palette of materials unifies the interior, demonstrating that, even in the most confined setting, glass has the potential to enrich and animate space.

Architects and designers whose work is featured in this book:

Azman Owens Architects

8, St. Alban's Place

London, N1 0NX

UK

tel. *+44 20 7354 2955*

fax. *+44 20 7354 2955*

www.azmanowens.com

Pages: 162–165

Bataille + ibens Design N.V.

Architects

Vekestraat 13 Bus 14

2000 Antwerp

Belgium

tel. *+32 3 231 3593*

fax. *+32 3 213 8639*

bataille.ibens@planetinternet.be

Pages: 1, 30–45

Simon Conder Associates

Architects & Designers

Nile Street Studios

8, Nile Street

London, N1 7RF

UK

tel. *+44 20 7251 2144*

fax. *+44 20 7251 2145*

simon@simonconder.co.uk

Pages: 171, 184–187

Sandy Davidson Design

Interior designer

1505, Viewsite Terrace

Los Angeles, CA 90069

fax. *320 659 2107*

SandSandD@aol.com

Pages: 102–103, 168–170, 180,

182–183

Rodolfo Dordoni

Architect

11, Via Solferino

20121 Milan

Italy

tel. *+39 02 866574*

fax. *+39 02 878581*

dordoni@tin.it

Pages: 104–113

Mark Guard Architects

161, Whitfield Street

London, W1T 5ET

UK

tel. *+44 20 7380 1199*

fax. *+44 20 7387 5441*

www.markguard.com

Pages: 166–167

William R. Hefner AIA

William Hefner Architect L.L.C.

5820, Wilshire Boulevard

Suite 601

Los Angeles, CA 90036

tel. *323 931 1365*

fax. *323 931 1368*

wh@williamhefner.com

www.williamhefner.com

Pages: 102–103, 168–170, 180,

182–183

Jestico & Whiles

Architects

1, Cobourg Square

London, NW1 2HP

UK

tel. *+44 20 7380 0382*

fax. *+44 20 7380 0511*

Pages: 84–91

Marmol Radziner + Associates,

Architecture and Construction

2902, Nebraska Avenue

Santa Monica, CA 90404

tel. *310 264 1814*

fax. *310 264 1817*

www.marmol-radziner.com

Pages: endpapers, 124–133

Rick Mather

Architect

123, Camden High Street

London, NW1 7JR

UK

tel. *+44 20 7284 1727*

fax. *+44 20 7267 7826*

rma@mather.demon.co.uk

Contact: Laura Parker, Public

Relations Manager

Pages: 114–123, 172–173, 181

Moore Ruble Yudell Architects

& Planners

933, Pico Boulevard

Santa Monica, CA 90405

tel. *310 450 1400*

fax. *310 450 1403*

Pages: 64–71

Ogawa/Depardon Architects

137, Varick Street, 4th floor

New York, NY 10013

tel. *212 627 7390*

fax. *212 627 9681*

ogawdep@aol.com

Pages: 134–143

Graham Phillips RIBA

Architect

Pages: 20–29

Alan Power Architects

5, Haydens Place

London, W11 1LY

UK

tel. *+44 20 7229 9375*

fax. *+44 20 7221 4172*

Pages: 174–179

Damien Roland

Architect

Agence du Centre

6, rue Clovis

45100 Orléans

France

Pages: 144–149

Mack Scogin Merrill Elam

Architects

Principal architects: Mack

Scogin and Merrill Elam

75, J.W. Dobbs Avenue, N.E.

Atlanta, GA 30303

tel. *404 525 6869*

fax. *404 525 7061*

Pages: 6–8, 62–63, 72–83, 92–101,

150–161

Ken Shuttleworth

Architect

Pages: 18–19, 52–61

Sidnam Petrone Gartner

Architects

Coty Sidnam, Bill Petrone and

Eric Gartner

136, West 21st Street

New York, NY 10011

tel. *212 366 5500*

fax. *212 366 6559*

sidnampetr@aol.com

www.spgarchitects.com

Pages: 46–51

Picture credits

Endpapers The Lew House, originally designed by Richard Neutra in 1958, architect and contractor Marmol Radziner + Associates, Architecture and Construction; **1** Mr & Mrs Brants-Voets' house near Brussels designed by Claire Bataille & Paul ibens, landscape architect Mrs Voets; **6–7** A Mountain House in Georgia designed by Mack Scogin Merrill Elam Architects; **8** Nomentana Residence in Maine designed by Mack Scogin Merrill Elam Architects; **10–11** photographer Alan Weintraub/Arcaid The Sheats-Goldstein House in Los Angeles designed by John Lautner; **12 a** photographer Scott Frances/Esto/Arcaid The Farnsworth House designed by Mies van der Rohe; **12 bl & br** photographer Michael Halberstadt/Arcaid, Maison Verre designed by Pierre Chareau; **12–13 main** photographer James Sinclair/Architectural Association, New Canaan designed by Philip Johnson; **14–15** photographer Alan Weintraub/Arcaid The Sheats Goldstein House in Los Angeles designed by John Lautner; **16 al & bl** RIBA/Hopkins House 1975–76 designed by Michael Hopkins & Partners; **16–17 ac** photographer ©Mathew Weinreb, imagefind.com; **17 ar & br** photographer Richard Bryant/Arcaid, House at Glenorie North Sydney designed by Glen Murcutt; **18–19** A house in Wiltshire designed by Ken Shuttleworth; **20–29** Skywood House near London designed by Graham Phillips; **30–37** A house near Antwerp designed by Claire Bataille & Paul ibens in collaboration with Lieven Langhor; **38–45** Mr & Mrs Brants-Voets' house near Brussels designed by Claire Bataille & Paul ibens, landscape architect Mrs Voets; **46–51** A house in Harrison, New York, designed by Sidnam Petrone Gartner Architects; **52–61** A house in Wiltshire designed by Ken Shuttleworth; **62–63** Nomentana Residence in Maine designed by Mack Scogin Merrill Elam Architects; **64–71** "The Peg Yorkin House" by Moore Ruble Yudell Architects & Planners. Principal in charge Buzz Yudell, Principal Designer John Ruble, Project Architect Marc Schoeplein; **72–83** Nomentana Residence in Maine designed by Mack Scogin Merrill Elam Architects; **84–91** Tom Jestico & Vivien Fowler's house in London, design team Tom Jestico & Vivien Fowler; **92–101** A Mountain House in Georgia designed by Mack Scogin Merrill Elam Architects; **102–103** Joan Barnett's house in West Hollywood, designed by William R. Heffner AIA, interior design by Sandy Davidson Design; **104–113** "Urban Retreat" private residence—project by Milanese architect Rodolfo Dordoni; **114–123** A house in London designed by Rick Mather Architects; **124–133** The Lew House, originally designed by Richard Neutra in 1958, architect and contractor Marmol Radziner + Associates, Architecture and Construction; **134–143** Upper East Side Townhouse in New York City designed by Ogawa/Depardon Architects; **144–149** An atelier in Paris designed by Damien Roland; **150–161** A house in Atlanta designed by Mack Scogin Merrill Elam Architects; **162–165** A house in London designed by Azman Owens Architects; **166–167** A house refurbishment in north London, Mark Guard Architects; **168–170** "The Jackee" and Elgin Charles House in California's Hollywood Hills, designed by William R. Heffner AIA, interior design by Sandy Davidson Design; **171** A loft apartment in London designed by Simon Conder Associates; **172–173** A house in London designed by Rick Mather Architects; **174–179** A house in London designed by Alan Power; **180** "The Jackee" and Elgin Charles House in California's Hollywood Hills, designed by William R. Heffner AIA, interior design by Sandy Davidson Design; **181** A house in London designed by Rick Mather Architects; **182–183** "The Jackee" and Elgin Charles House in California's Hollywood Hills, designed by William R. Heffner AIA, interior design by Sandy Davidson Design; **184–187** A loft apartment in London designed by Simon Conder Associates.

Index

FIGURES IN *ITALICS* REFER TO CAPTIONS

Acknowledgments

Thanks are due to all the architects and designers who provided source material for this book. Thanks are also due to my colleagues on *The Architectural Review* and to the editorial team at Ryland Peters & Small for heroic reserves of patience and support.

To my partner Malcolm Frost, *un grazie di cuore*.

The publishers would like to thank everyone who allowed us to photograph their homes for this book.